CONCISE COLLEGE TEXTS

FAMILY LAW

OTHER BOOKS IN THIS SERIES:

Tort, by C. D. Baker
"O" Level Law, by W. J. Brown
Press Law, by Robin Callender Smith
Contract, by F. R. Davies
Sale of Goods and Consumer Credit, by A. P. Dobson
Labour Law, by C. D. Drake
The English Legal System, by K. J. Eddey
Hotel and Catering Law, by David Field
Law of Arbitration, by W. H. Gill
Land Law, by W. Swinfen Green and N. Henderson
Shipping Law, by Robert Grime
Introduction to Commercial Law, by C. Hamblin and F.B. Wright
The Law and Procedure of Meetings, by M. Moore
General Principles of Law, by C. R. Newton
Criminal Law, by P. Seago
Construction Law, by J. Uff
Patents, Trade Marks, Copyright and Industrial Designs,
    T. A. Blanco White and Robin Jacob

AUSTRALIA
The Law Book Company Ltd.
Sydney : Melbourne : Brisbane

CANADA AND U.S.A.
The Carswell Company Ltd.
Agincourt, Ontario

INDIA
N. M. Tripathi Private Ltd.
Bombay
and
Eastern Law House Private Ltd.
Calcutta *and* Delhi
M.P.P. House
Bangalore

ISRAEL
Steimatzky's Agency Ltd.
Jerusalem : Tel Aviv : Haifa

MALAYSIA : SINGAPORE : BRUNEI
Malayan Law Journal (Pte.) Ltd.
Singapore

NEW ZEALAND
Sweet & Maxwell (N.Z.) Ltd.
Auckland

PAKISTAN
Pakistan Law House
Karachi

CONCISE COLLEGE TEXTS

GRANT AND LEVIN:
FAMILY LAW

FOURTH EDITION

by

JENNIFER LEVIN, LL.B., LL.M.
Solicitor,
Co-Director, Legal Action Group

LONDON
SWEET & MAXWELL
1982

First Edition 1970
Second Edition 1973
Third Edition 1977
Second Impression 1979
Fourth Edition 1982

Published by
Sweet & Maxwell Limited of
11 New Fetter Lane, London
Printed in Great Britain by
Richard Clay (The Chaucer Press) Limited,
Bungay, Suffolk

British Library Cataloguing in Publication Data

Grant, Brian
    Family law.—4th ed.—(Concise college texts).
    1. Domestic relations—England
    I. Title   II. Levin, Jennifer   III. Series
    344.2061'5   KD750

ISBN 0–421–30240–2
ISBN 0–421–28280–0 Pbk

AUTHOR'S PREFACE TO FOURTH EDITION

A fourth edition of this book since its first appearance in 1970 confirms its value as a readable and reliable primer of family law. Miss Jennifer Levin has once again undertaken the task of editorship which should ensure the book's continuing popularity and usefulness.

Her name is henceforth twinned with mine as a deserved acknowledgment of her contribution to the book's lasting success.

Tunbridge Wells   BRIAN GRANT
1982

EDITOR'S PREFACE TO FOURTH EDITION

FAMILY law is in a constant state of change but it does not always change in ways anticipated by legislators or even judges. Only a decade ago the legislature, when the new law of divorce was enacted, was concerned to protect wives from "Casanova" husbands and from financial destitution on divorce. Now the emphasis is on the need for wives to be economically independent of their divorced husbands and the majority of petitioners for divorce are women, not men. The Law Commission has, once again, undertaken a review of the laws on maintenance.

The pace of legislative change in family law has slowed down considerably since the last edition of this book although there are a number of statutes which, either directly or indirectly, have introduced major changes (*e.g.* the Domestic Proceedings and Magistrates' Courts Act 1978, Housing Act 1980, Child Care Act 1980, Social Security Act 1980 and Matrimonial Homes and Property Act 1981). More significant than legislative changes, however, have been the changes in approach and emphasis that are reflected in the everyday concerns of families, their legal advisers and the courts. The general introduction of the "Special" divorce procedure, the consequential changes in legal aid and the fact that only 2 per cent. of divorces are now defended means that the substantive law on divorce is less important—certainly there have been no significant developments in this area since the last edition of this book. On the other hand there have been numerous interesting developments in the law on financial provision on divorce as the courts try to come to grips with the changing role of women and the needs of children. Should a "clean break" be favoured or should ex-wives expect a "meal ticket for life"? Should the spouse who gets the children also get the home? What should the relationship be between private maintenance obligations and public provision via social security? Other social issues have been the concern of both legislation and judges. Should unmarried cohabitants be treated like married couples? What should the courts do about domestic violence? How should couples be treated by the tax and social security laws? What rights do children and parents have where children are taken into local authority care?

These changes in emphasis have required much of this book to be rearranged and rewritten, just as changes in the law have required that it be extensively revised. New sections (*e.g.* on domestic violence, tax, and social security) have been introduced and others (on children) expanded. Some (on divorce and nullity) have been contracted. The aim is to provide a short, clear and readable account of the law relating to the family that will be useful to both law student and layperson, in particular those advising clients on the problems arising from marriage breakdown.

The law is stated as at March 1982.

LONDON   JENNIFER LEVIN
March 1982

CONTENTS

Author's Preface to Fourth Edition   v
Editor's Preface to Fourth Edition   vii
Table of Cases   xi
Table of Statutes   xvii

Part One: Marriage

Introduction   1
1. Marriage   3
2. Husband and Wife   16

Part Two: Breakdown of Marriage

Introduction   43
3. Immediate Problems and Emergency Remedies   45
4. Separation Agreements   51
5. Matrimonial Orders in the Magistrates' Courts   54
6. Divorce and Judicial Separation   63
7. Nullity   79
8. Financial and Property Orders on Marriage Breakdown   87
9. Recognition of Foreign Decrees   100

Part Three: Children

10. Parental Rights, Custody and Guardianship   105
11. Illegitimacy and Legitimation   114
12. Wardship   120
13. Adoption   124
14. Children in Need   133

Index   141

TABLE OF CASES

A. *v.* A. [1974] 1 All E.R. 755 96
—— *v.* Liverpool City Council [1981] 2 W.L.R. 948 .... 122, 133, 135, 137
Adams *v.* Adams [1951] 1 K.B. 536 53
—— *v.* —— (1978) 122 S.J. 348 92
Adamson *v.* Adamson (1907) 23 T.L.R. 434 70
Adeos *v.* Adeoso [1980] 1 W.L.R. 1535 47
Armitage *v.* Att.-Gen. [1906] P. 135 101
Armstrong *v.* Armstrong (1974) 118 S.J. 579 90
Attwood *v.* Attwood [1968] P. 591 92

B., *Re* [1975] Fam. 127 128
——, *Re, The Times,* August 8, 1981 .... 106, 122
—— *v.* —— (B. (An Infant) intervening) [1971] 1 W.L.R. 1486 109
Baindail *v.* Baindail [1946] P. 122 12
Balfour *v.* Balfour [1919] 2 K.B. 571 39
Bamgbose *v.* Daniel [1955] A.C. 107 12
Banik *v.* Banik [1973] 1 W.L.R. 860 74
Bassett *v.* Bassett [1975] Fam. 76 46
Bastable *v.* Bastable [1968] 1 W.L.R. 1684 66
Baxter *v.* Baxter [1948] A.C. 274 81
Beaumont, *Re* [1980] 1 All E.R. 266 36
Bedson *v.* Bedson [1965] 2 Q.B. 666 26
Beeken *v.* Beeken [1948] P. 302 70
Berry *v.* Humm & Co. [1915] 1 K.B. 627 38
Best *v.* Fox (Samuel) & Co. Ltd. [1952] A.C. 716 .... 16, 17
Billington *v.* Billington [1974] Fam. 24 60
Bishop, *Re* [1965] Ch. 450 28
Blackwell *v.* Blackwell [1943] 2 All E.R. 579 29
Bowman *v.* Bowman [1949] P. 353 64
Brickell *v.* Brickell [1974] Fam. 74
Buckland *v.* Buckland [1968] P. 297 83

C., *Re* [1964] 3 All E.R. 483 135
—— *v.* C. [1979] 2 W.L.R. 95 64
C. (M.A.), *Re* [1966] 1 W.L.R. 646 119
Carr *v.* Carr [1974] 1 All E.R. 1193 .... 66, 67
Carson *v.* Carson (1981) 125 S.J. 513 97
Chalcroft *v.* Chalcroft [1969] 1 W.L.R. 1612 68
Chapman *v.* Chapman [1969] 1 W.L.R. 1367 23
Chipchase *v.* Chipchase [1942] P. 37 11

Clare, Re [1981] 1 All E.R. 16 122
Cleary v. Cleary [1974] 1 W.L.R. 73 66
Cole, Re [1964] Ch. 175 29
Coleman v. Coleman [1973] Fam. 10 ....88, 92
Colin Smith Music v. Ridge [1975] 1 W.L.R. 463 28
Cooke v. Head [1972] 1 W.L.R. 518 ....11, 24
Cooper v. Crane [1891] P. 369 82

D., Re (1976) Fam. 185 122
——, Re [1977] A.C. 607 129
——, Re [1977] Fam. 158 122
D. (An Infant), Re [1959] 1 Q.B. 229 125
D.X., Re [1949] Ch. 320 125
Davies v. Taylor (No. 2) [1974] A.C. 225 38
Davis v. Johnson [1978] 2 W.L.R. 182; affirmed [1979] A.C. 264 ...... 46, 47
Day v. Day [1980] Fam. 29 76
Dennis v. Dennis [1955] P. 153 65
De Reneville v. De Reneville [1948] P. 100 79
Din v. N.A.B. [1967] 2 Q.B. 213 14
Dipper v. Dipper [1981] Fam. 31.................................. 91, 98, 107
Draskovic v. Draskovic (1980) 125 S.J. 306 97
Dyson v. Fox [1975] 3 W.L.R. 744 11

E., Re [1964] 1 W.L.R. 51 122
——, Re [1967] Ch. 761; affirming [1967] Ch. 287 123
Elsworth v. Elsworth [1979] 9 Fam. Law 21 47
Ette v. Ette [1964] 1 W.L.R. 1433 92
Evers' Trust, Re; Papps v. Evers [1980] 1 W.L.R. 1327 21
Eves v. Eves [1975] 1 W.L.R. 1338....................................11, 24

F., Re [1969] 2 Ch. 239 108
——, Re [1976] 2 W.L.R. 189 109
Fitzpatrick v. Fitzpatrick (1979) 9 Fam. Law 16 94
Flynn decd., Re [1968] 1 W.L.R. 103 15
Foley v. Foley [1981] 3 W.L.R. 284 91
Furniss v. Furniss (1981) The Times, 2 October 90

G. v. M. (1885) 10 App.Cas. 171 85
Gaines v. W. [1968] 1 Q.B. 782 117
Gandolfo v. Gandolfo (Standard Chartered Bank, Garnshee [1981]
    Q.B. 359.. 88
Gollins v. Gollins [1964] A.C. 644 67
Goodrich v. Goodrich [1971] 1 W.L.R. 1142 66

H., Re (1980) 10 Fam. Law 248 109
Harding v. Harding (1979) 10 Fam. Law 146 47
Hardy v. Hardy (1981) 125 S.J. 463 92

Harnett v. Harnett [1974] 1 W.L.R. 219 90
Haroutunian v. Jennings (1977) 121 S.J. 663 118
Harriman v. Harriman [1909] P. 123 70
Harrods Ltd., v. Tester [1937] 2 All E.R. 236 29
Harthan v. Harthan [1949] P. 115 81
Hawkins v. Att.-Gen. [1966] 1 W.L.R. 978 115
Hazell v. Hazell [1972] 1 W.L.R. 301 23
Hewer v. Bryant [1969] 3 W.L.R. 428 107
Hopes v. Hopes [1949] P. 227 69
Hulley v. Thompson [1981] 1 W.L.R. 159 95
Hyde v. Hyde (1866) L.R. 1 P. & D. 3, 12
Hyman v. Hyman [1929] A.C. 601 52

J., Re [1973] Fam. 106 131
—— v. C. [1970] A.C. 668 108
J.S. (A Minor), Re [1981] Fam. 22 116
Jelley v. Iliffe [1981] 2 W.L.R. 801 .... 36, 37
Jodla v. Jodla [1960] 1 W.L.R. 236 82
Jones v. Challenger [1901] 1 Q.B. 176 26
—— v. Jones [1976] Fam. 8 90
—— v. Maynard [1951] 1 Ch. 572 28
Joseph v. Joseph [1953] 1 W.L.R. 1182 70
Joyce v. Joyce and O'Hare (1979) Fam. 93 101
Jussa v. Jussa [1972] 1 W.L.R. 881 110

K., Re [1965] 1 W.L.R. 802 120
——, Re [1972] 3 All E.R. 769 172
—— v. J.M.P. Co. [1975] 2 W.L.R. 457 38
Katz v. Katz [1972] 1 W.L.R. 955 67
Khan v. Khan [1980] 1 W.L.R. 355 91
Kirkham v. Boughey [1958] 2 Q.B. 338 17
Kokosinski v. Kokosinski [1980] Fam. 72 91
Krishnan v. London Borough of Sutton [1970] Ch. 181 135
Krystman v. Krystman [1973] 1 W.L.R. 927 91

L., Re [1974] 1 W.L.R. 250 123
L. (A.C.) (An Infant), Re [1971] 3 All E.R. 743 122
Langston, In the Estate of [1953] P. 100 33
Lewis v. Lewis [1978] 1 All E.R. 729 48
Lewisham London Borough Council v. Lewisham Juvenile Court
    Justices [1980] A.C. 273 .... 135, 136

M., Re [1968] P. 174 52
——, Re (1980) 10 Fam. Law 184 96
—— v. J. (1977) 8 Fam. Law 12 119
—— v. M. [1973] 2 All E.R. 81 109
McCartney v. McCartney [1981] Fam. 59 49
McLean v. Nugent (1979) 123 S.J. 521 47

Macey *v.* Macey (1981) 11 Fam. Law 248 92
Mahadervan *v.* Mahadervan [1964] P. 233 10
Malyon *v.* Plummer [1964] 1 Q.B. 330 35
Masich *v.* Masich (1977) 7 Fam. Law 245 46
Mason *v.* Mason [1972] Fam. 302 71
Matcham *v.* Matcham (1976) 120 S.J. 570 71
Mathias *v.* Mathias [1972] Fam. 287 72
Mesher *v.* Mesher and Hall (Note) [1980] 1 All E.R. 126 97
Meyer, *Re* [1971] P. 298 101
Meyrick's Settlement, *Re* [1921] 1 Ch. 311 51
Milne *v.* Milne (1981) 125 S.J. 375 88
Minton *v.* Minton [1979] A.C. 593 51
Mohamed *v.* Knott [1969] 1 Q.B. 1 4
Moore *v.* Moore, *The Times,* May 10, 1980 91

NATIONAL ASSISTANCE BOARD *v.* Parkes [1955] 2 Q.B. 506 33
National Provincial Bank *v.* Ainsworth [1965] A.C. 1175 25
—— *v.* Hastings Car Mart [1964] Ch. 665 99
Nixon *v.* Nixon [1969] 1 W.L.R. 1676 23

O'CONNOR *v.* A. & B. [1971] 1 W.L.R. 1227 128
O'Dare Ai *v.* Glamorgan (1980) 10 Fam. Law 215 136
O'Neill *v.* O'Neill [1975] 1 W.L.R. 1118 67

P., *Re* [1962] 1 W.L.R. 1296 129
——, *Re* [1977] 1 All E.R. 182 128
Padolecchia *v.* Padolecchia (*orse.* Leis) [1968] P. 314 13
Pardy *v.* Pardy [1939] P. 288... 53, 70
Park, *In the Estate of* [1954] P. 112 84
Parker *v.* Parker [1972] Fam. 116 72
Pascoe *v.* Turner [1979] 1 W.L.R. 431 24
Payne-Collins *v.* Taylor Woodrow [1975] Q.B. 300 38
Pettit *v.* Pettit [1963] P. 177 81
Pettitt *v.* Pettitt [1970] A.C. 777... 20, 21, 22, 24
Pheasant *v.* Pheasant [1972] Fam. 202 67
Potter *v.* Potter [1975] 5 Fam. Law 161 82

QUAZI *v.* Quazi [1980] A.C. 744; reversing [1979] 3 W.L.R. 402;
    reversing (1978) 8 Fam. Law 203... 100

R. *v.* Bow Road Domestic Proceedings Court, *ex p.* Adedigba [1968] 2
    Q.B. 572 117
—— *v.* Gould [1968] 2 Q.B. 65 6
—— *v.* Halifax Justices, *ex p.* Woolveston (1978) 123 S.J. 80 57
—— *v.* Jackson [1891] 1 Q.B. 671 16
—— *v.* Oxford City Justices [1975] Q.B. 1 137
—— *v.* Registrar General, *ex p.* Minhas [1976] 2 W.L.R. 475 100
—— *v.* Tolson (1889) 23 Q.B.D. 168 6

R. (Adoption), *Re* [1967] 1 W.L.R. 34 127
Radwan *v*. Radwan [1973] Fam. 24 13
Rashid *v*. Rashid (1979) 9 Fam. Law 118 109
Rawlings *v*. Rawlings [1964] P. 398 26
Reiterbund *v*. Reiterbund [1975] Fam. 99 74
Redpath *v*. Redpath [1950] W.N. 148 65
Regan *v*. Regan [1977] 1 W.L.R. 84 98
Rennick *v*. Rennick [1977] 1 W.L.R. 1455 46
Richards *v*. Dove [1974] 1 All E.R. 888 24
Richards *v*. Richards [1972] 1 W.L.R. 1073 67
Rimmer *v*. Rimmer [1953] 1 Q.B. 63 23
Roberts *v*. Roberts [1970] P. 1 92
Rodewald *v*. Rodewald [1977] 2 W.L.R. 191 92
Roper *v*. Roper [1972] 1 W.L.R. 1314 66
Ross *v*. Pearson [1976] 1 W.L.R. 224 59
Rukat *v*. Rukat [1975] Fam. 63 74

S., *Re* [1965] 1 W.L.R. 483 135
——, *Re* [1976] Fam. 1 131
——, *Re* (1978) 9 Fam. Law 88 64
—— *v*. McC. (formerly S.) and M. (S. intervening) [1970] 1 W.L.R.
    672; [1970] 1 All E.R. 1162 116
—— *v*. —— [1968] P. 185 95
—— *v*. —— (1976) 6 Fam. Law 148 108
—— *v*. —— *orse*. C. [1956] P. 1 81
—— *v*. —— *orse*. W. [1963] P. 162............... 81
Samson *v*. Samson [1960] 1 W.L.R. 190 29
Santos *v*. Santos [1972] Fam. 247 71
Sapsford *v*. Sapsford [1954] P. 394 65
Shallow *v*. Shallow [1979] Fam. 1 94
Sharpe *v*. Sharpe (1981) 11 Fam. Law 121 89
Singh *v*. Singh [1971] P. 226 83
Slater *v*. Slater [1953] P. 235 85
Smith *v*. Smith [1948] P. 77 85
Spindlow *v*. Spindlow [1979] Ch. 52 46
Stringfellow *v*. Stringfellow [1976] 1 W.L.R. 645 68
Szechter *v*. Szechter [1971] P. 286 83

T., *Re* [1968] 1 Ch. 704 123
T.L.R. *v*. Essex County Council (1978) 9 Fam. Law 15 138
Talbot *v*. Talbot (1971) 115 S.J. 870 73
Tanner *v*. Tanner [1975] 1 W.L.R. 1346 12
Thompson *v*. Thompson [1976] Fam. 25 ....27, 98
Thurlow *v*. Thurlow [1976] Fam. 32 68
Tilley *v*. London Borough of Wandsworth [1981] 1 All E.R. 1162 134
Tinker *v*. Tinker [1970] P. 136 30

Tulley v. Tulley [1965] 109 S.J. 956, C.A. 23
Turczak v. Turczak [1970] P. 198 102

VALIER v. Valier (1925) 133 L.T. 830 84

W., Re [1964] Ch. 202 106
——, Re [1971] A.C. 682 128
—— v. W. [1952] P. 152 85
—— v. —— (1971) 115 S.J. 93 95
W. (R.J.) v. W. (S.J.) [1972] Fam. 152 110
Wachtel v. Wachtel [1973] 2 W.L.R. 84 ....57, 89, 90, 92
Walker v. Walker [1978] 1 W.L.R. 533 46
Warden v. Warden [1981] 3 W.L.R. 435 53
Watson v. Nikolaisen [1955] 2 Q.B. 286 127
West v. West [1978] Fam., 1 90
Wheatley v. Waltham Forest London Borough Council [1980] A.C.
    311 136
Wilkinson (decd.), Re [1978] 3 W.L.R. 514 37
Williams v. Williams [1963] A.C. 698 67
—— v. —— [1977] 1 All E.R. 28 26
Williams v. Williams (1981) 11 Fam. Law 23 92
Williams & Glyn's Bank v. Boland and Brown [1981] A.C. 487;
    affirming [1979] Ch. 312 27
Winter v. Winter [1942] P. 151 64
Wright v. Wright [1976] Fam. 114 75

X., Re [1975] 1 All E.R. 697 121

TABLE OF STATUTES

1837 Willis Act (7 Will. 4 & 1
      Vict. c. 26)—
      s. 18 33

1861 Offences against the
      Person Act (24 &
      25 Vict. c. 100)—
      s. 57 6

1882 Married Women's Prop-
      erty Act (45 & 46
      Vict. c. 75)—
      s. 17 .... 3, 20, 21

1925 Administration of
      Estates Act (15 &
      16 Geo. 5, c. 23) 33
      s. 55(1)(x) 33
      Law of Property Act (15
      & 16 Geo. 5,
      c. 20)—
      ss. 52(1), 53(1)(b)(c)   29
      s. 177 33
      Land Registration Act
      (15 & 16 Geo. 5,
      c. 86)—
      s. 70(g) 27
      Criminal Justice Act (15
      & 16 Geo. 5,
      c. 86)—
      s. 47 40

1926 Legitimacy Act (16 &
      17 Geo. 5, c. 60) 114

1929 Age of Marriage Act (19
      & 20 Geo. 5, c. 36)   4

1933 Children and Young
      Persons Act (23 &
      24 Geo. 5, c. 12)—
      s. 1 106
      s. 3 106
      s. 5 106
      Sched. 1 138

1935 Law Reform (Married
      Women and Tort-
      feasors) Act (25 &
      26 Geo. 5, c. 30) 39

1937 Matrimonial Causes
      Act (1 Edw. 8 & 1
      Geo. 6, c. 57) 81

1938 Inheritance (Family
      Provision) Act (1 &
      2 Geo. 6, c. 45) 34
      Marriage Act (12, 13 &
      14 Geo. 6, c. 76) 12
      ss. 25, 49 10
      Sched. 1 5
      Sched. 2 .... 7, 8
      Intestate's Estates Act
      (15 & 16 Geo. 6 &
      1 Eliz. 2, c. 64) 33, 34
      Sched. 2 34

1957 Affiliation Proceedings
      Act (5 & 6 Eliz. 2,
      c. 55) 117

1958 Matrimonial Causes
      (Property and
      Maintenance) Act
      (6 & 7 Eliz. 2,
      c. 35)—
      s. 7 21
      Maintenance Orders
      Act (6 & 7 Eliz. 2,
      c. 39) 59
      s. 16 60
      Adoption Act (7 & 8
      Eliz. 2, c. 5) 124, 125

1960 Marriage (Enabling)
      Act (8 & 9 Eliz. 2,
      c. 29) 5
      Adoption Act (8 & 9
      Eliz. 2, c. 59) 124
      s. 1(1) 124

1962 Law Reform (Husband and Wife) Act (10 & 11 Eliz. 2, c. 48) 40

1964 Married Women's Property Act (c. 19) 29
Adoption Act (c. 57) 124

1966 Family Provision Act (c. 35) 33

1967 Matrimonial Homes Act (c. 56) 12, 25, 26
s. 1 .... 27, 28, 45
ss. 3–6 25
s. 7 ....27, 98
Adoption Act (c. 53) 124
Theft Act (c. 60)—
s. 30(2) 40
(3)–(4) 40, 41
Civil Evidence Act (c. 64)—
s. 16(3) 41

1969 Family Law Reform Act (c. 46) 33
s. 5(2) 118
s. 7 121
Part III 115
s. 26 115
Sched. 3, para. 3(1) 120
Children and Young Persons Act (c. 54) 134
s. 1 137
(1) 138
(2)(a)–(c) 175
s. 2(2) 138
(12) 139
s. 4 173
ss. 11–19 139
ss. 20, 21, 24 139
s. 28 137
Divorce Reform Act (c. 55).......54, 63, 65, 74, 90

1970 Income and Corporation Taxes Act (c. 10)—
s. 37 30
s. 65 94

1970 Administration of Justice Act (c. 13)—
s. 12 60
Law Reform (Miscellaneous Provisions) Act (c. 33)—
s. 4 16
s. 5(a), (c) 17
Matrimonial Proceedings and Property Act (c. 45)—
s. 20 16
s. 37 24
s. 39 21
s. 41 18

1971 Guardianship of Minors Act (c. 3) 137
s. 1 108
s. 3 112
s. 4 112
s. 5 112
s. 6 112
s. 7 107
s. 9 118
(2) 137
s. 10 112
Attachment of Earnings Act (c. 32) 59
s. 3(1)(5), 6(5) 59
s. 9(4), 15 60
Nullity of Marriage Act (c. 44)—
s. 5 79
Recognition of Divorces and Legal Separations Act (c. 53) 100
s. 3(1) 100
s. 5(1) 100
(2) 100
s. 6(a) 101
s. 8(2) 101
(3) 102
Finance Act (c. 68)—
s. 23 31

1972 Maintenance Orders (Reciprocal Enforcement) Act (c. 18) 102

Matrimonial Proceedings (Polygamous Marriages) Act (c. 38) 13
    s. 3 13

Finance Act (c. 41)—
    s. 75 31

Housing Finance Act (c. 47) 11

Affiliation Proceedings (Amendment) Act (c. 49) 118
    s. 1 118

1973 Matrimonial Causes Act (c. 18) 97
    s. 1 ....65, 77
       (2)(b) 68
       (d) 71
       (3) 72
    s. 2(1) 66
       (3) 68
       (5) 69, 71
       (6) 70
       (7) 71
    s. 3 63
       (3) 64
    s. 5 72
    s. 6(2) 64
    s. 7 76
    s. 8(1) 128
    s. 9(2) 77
    s. 10(1)...................71, 77
       (2)–(4) 75
    s. 11(a) 4
       (b) 80
       (c) 4, 80
       (d) 80
    ss. 11–16 79
    s. 12(b) 81
       (c) 82
    s. 13 85
    s. 16 ....79, 114
    s. 17(2)..................77, 78

1973 Matrimonial Clauses Act—cont.
    s. 19 6
    s. 20 72
    ss. 21–24.................... 80
    s. 22 87
    s. 23 ....20, 26, 88, 92
       (2) 119
    s. 24 ....20, 26, 27, 88, 97
    s. 25 .... 56, 89, 90
       (1) 88
       (2)(3) 96, 97
    s. 27 .... 23, 75, 90
    s. 28 88
    s. 29 96
    s. 31 ....92, 98
       (5)(6) 98
    s. 34(19 52
    s. 35 ....51, 52
    s. 36 52
    s. 37 99
    s. 41 .... 74, 78, 110
    s. 42 ....121, 125
       (1) 111
    ss. 43, 44 .... 109, 110
    s. 45 117
    s. 48(2) 86
    s. 52 ....95, 110
       (1) 119

Guardianship Act (c. 29) 135
    s. 1 ....105, 107
       (2) 52
    s. 2(2) 109

Domicile and Matrimonial Proceedings Act (c. 45) 123
    s. 1 14
    s. 3 14
    s. 5(2) 123
       (4) 11
    s. 16 100

1975 Social Security Act (c. 14)—
    ss. 44, 47, 66 32
    s. 162(b) 13

1975 Inheritance (Provision
      for Family and
      Dependants) Act
      (c. 63)...................11, 34
      s. 1(1)(e) 35, 37
         (2) 35
         (3) 35, 37
      s. 3(2) 35
      s. 5 36
      s. 19(2) 36
      Children Act (c. 72) 112,
                  124, 126, 127,
                        129, 140
      s. 1 130
      s. 3...................... 128, 130
      s. 4 172
      s. 8 132
         (7) 131
      s. 9 126
      s. 11 125
      s. 12 126
      s. 13 126
      s. 14 129
      s. 20 131
      s. 26 132
      s. 33 92
         (3) 113
      s. 34 113
      s. 37(1) 125
      s. 41 113
      s. 85(1) 105
         (2) 107
         (3) 107

1976 Fatal Accidents Act (c.
      30)................. 12, 17, 37
      s. 1 37
      ss. 4, 5 38
      s. 107(1) 119
      Legitimacy   Act   (c.
      31)—
      ss. 1, 2 114
      s. 5 34
      Adoption Act (c. 36) 124
      s. 5 132
      s. 6...................... 128, 130
      s. 7 126
      s. 12(6) 131
      s. 13 126

1976 Adoption Act—cont.
      s. 15 125
         (3) 125
      s. 16 126
      s. 17 132
      s. 18 129
      s. 51 167
      s. 52 124
      s. 65 131
      s. 65 166
      Domestic Violence and
      Matrimonial Pro-
      ceedings Act (c. 50) 11,
                        28, 46
      s. 1(2) 47
      s. 2(1) 48
      s. 3 25
      Supplementary Benefits
      Act (c. 71)—
      s. 18 32
1977 Housing (Homeless Per-
      sons) Act (c. 48) 11, 47
1978 Domestic   Proceedings
      and   Magistrates'
      Courts Act (c. 22) 54, 55
      s. 1..........................19, 55
      s. 2 57
      s. 3....................56, 57
      s. 4 58
      s. 6 55
      s. 7 55
      s. 8................. 57, 58, 111
      s. 9 57
      s. 10 ....57, 109
      s. 11 57
      s. 12 111
      s. 13 58
      s. 14 58
      ss. 16–18 48
      s. 20 58
      s. 25 19
      s. 50(2)................ 117, 118
      s. 78(1)....................49, 60
1980 Child Care Act (c. 5) 122,
                        133, 134
      s. 1.......................133, 134
      s. 2........122, 134, 135, 136
      s. 3......................135, 136

1980 Child Care Act—*cont.*
    s. 7 137
    s. 13 135
    s. 18 133
Foster Children Act
    (c. 6) 133
Magistrates' Courts
    Act (c. 43)—
    s. 32(1) 58
    s. 82 61
    s. 95 ....58, 60

1980 Housing Act (c. 51)....... 11,
    27, 28, 98

1981 Matrimonial Homes
    and Property Act
    (c. 24) 97
    s. 2 26
    s. 6 27
    s. 7 87
    s. 8 98

PART I
MARRIAGE

INTRODUCTION

Much of the law relating to the family has been created as a response to the disputes and problems that have arisen in the context of the creation and breakdown of marriage. Textbooks on family law tend to begin with the law on the creation of a marriage, and the consequent obligations of the spouses towards each other, and then consider the law on separation and divorce. This book is no exception. However, to the non-lawyer the family has a wider connotation. He will think first of the children and of their upbringing, whereas the law often treats children as "ancillaries" to the disputes of their parents. He will be concerned with the position of a wider network of persons than the married couple—grand-parents, aunts, uncles, brothers, sisters, step-parents, etc. He will also be concerned with couples who live together without being married.

Throughout this book the traditional arrangement of subject-matter—marriage, breakdown of marriage and children—is re-tained. But within this framework we will also consider, where appropriate, the position of other members of the family, especially where disputes over children are concerned. The legal position of cohabitants will also be examined and contrasted with that applicable to married couples.

CHAPTER 1

MARRIAGE

The classic legal definition of marriage in English law was formulated by Lord Penzance in *Hyde* v. *Hyde* (1866):

> "I conceive that marriage as understood in Christendom, may . . . be defined as the voluntary union for life of one man and one woman to the exclusion of all others . . . "

Although this definition no longer rigorously applies when the validity of the foreign marriage is in question (see *post*, p.12), it undoubtedly continues to be important in relation to marriages celebrated in England and to persons domiciled in England (see p.14 for further details on domicile). Such marriages must be heterosexual, monogamous, intended to be lifelong and voluntarily contracted by parties having the capacity so to contract. In addition certain formalities, either civil or religious, must be complied with. All these features will be examined in more detail below. First, however, the legal position of those "engaged" to be married must be examined.

1. Engagements

A promise to marry, duly accepted, used to create a binding contract which, if broken without lawful excuse, could give rise to a claim for damages for "breach of promise." Such actions had long fallen into disuse before they were abolished by the Law Reform (Miscellaneous Provisions) Act 1970, section 1 of which provides:

> "An agreement between two persons to marry one another shall not . . . have effect as a contract giving rise to legal rights and no action shall lie . . . for breach of such an agreement . . . "

This does not mean that a promise to marry is totally devoid of any legal consequences. Sections 2 and 3 of the above Act make special provision concerning the property relationships of couples where an engagement is terminated. If a dispute over ownership or possession of property arises then the same informal proceedings for settling it (*i.e.* under the Married Womens' Property Act 1882, s.17 as amended; see p.20) apply as in the case of a husband and wife, provided the proceedings are begun within three years of the termination of the engagement (1970 Act, s.2(2)).

Section 3 of the 1970 Act deals with engagement gifts. The basic rule is that where one party makes a gift to the other on the condition (express or implied) that it should be returned if the engagement is ended, the gift must be returned even at the request of the party responsible for terminating the agreement to marry. The exception to this rule concerns the engagement ring; strangely, it is presumed that this is intended to be an absolute gift. Its return can be demanded only if it is proved that it was given on the condition that it should be returned if the marriage did not take place (1970 Act, s.3(2)), a condition likely to be difficult to establish in view of the circumstances in which most engagement rings are given. It should be noted that a fiancé has no legal remedy if he or she has spent money in preparation for the wedding or marriage which is wasted when the engagement is terminated. Thus no compensation can be obtained for wasted expenditure made for a wedding reception or to obtain living accommodation which is no longer required. What the 1970 Act does not do is define "an agreement to marry." Presumably its provisions will apply only if *both* parties have both the capacity to marry and to make a contract (*e.g.* be over 18 (not 16) and unmarried).

2. Capacity to marry
To contract a valid marriage in English law both parties must be:

(a) *Of opposite sex*
There can be no valid marriage between persons of the same sex (Matrimonial Causes Act 1973, s. 11(*c*)). Whether or not a person is male or female will depend on medical evidence but the courts will be very unwilling to regard a person who was born a male as having become a female (or vice versa) as a result of a sex change operation. In *Corbett* v. *Corbett* (1971) a man who had undergone an operation and then lived as a woman was held on the evidence not to be a woman biologically and therefore incapable of contracting a valid marriage with a man.

(b) *Over sixteen years of age*
Since 1929 (Age of Marriage Act) the minimum age for a legally valid marriage has been 16 for both sexes (previously it was 14 for a boy and 12 for a girl). A marriage celebrated under the age of 16 is void (Matrimonial Causes Act 1973, s. 11 (*a*)) and cannot become valid simply by continuing to live as man and wife after the age of 16. Where a marriage is celebrated abroad by parties whose domiciliary law permits marriages at a younger age, the marriage will be recognised as valid in English law (*Mohamed* v. *Knott* (1969)).

(c) *Not within the prohibited degrees of consanguinity and affinity*

Marriages between persons within certain prohibited degrees of consanguinity (blood relationship) or affinity (relationship by marriage) are void. These have changed in detail over the years; in general, the categories of persons whose marriage is forbidden have been narrowed down, though a recent attempt to permit marriage between a man and his deceased wife's daughter (*i.e.* his step-daughter) failed to get through Parliament. The prevailing table of "prohibited degrees of kindred and affinity" is set out in the Marriage Act 1949, Sched. 1, as amended by the Marriage (Enabling) Act 1960, and lists the persons that a man or woman may not marry as follows:

Mother	Father
Daughter	Son
Father's mother	Father's father
Mother's mother	Mother's father
Son's daughter	Son's son
Daughter's daughter	Daughter's son
Sister	Brother
Wife's mother	Husband's father
Wife's daughter	Husband's son
Father's wife	Mother's husband
Son's wife	Daughter's husband
Father's father's wife	Father's mother's husband
Mother's father's wife	Mother's mother's husband
Wife's father's mother	Husband's father's father
Wife's mother's mother	Husband's mother's father
Wife's son's daughter	Husband's son's son
Wife's daughter's daughter	Husband's daughter's son
Son's son's wife	Son's daughter's husband
Daughter's son's wife	Daughter's daughter's husband
Father's sister	Father's brother
Mother's sister	Mother's brother
Brother's daughter	Brother's son
Sister's daughter	Sister's son

These prohibitions cover both legitimate and illegitimate issue and relationships of both half and full blood. An adopted child remains within the prohibited degrees in relation to his *natural* family and is also unable to marry his *adoptive* parents. He can, however, marry his adoptive parents' children, *i.e.* his adoptive sisters or brothers.

(d) *Unmarried*

A second marriage celebrated whilst a valid first marriage still subsists is void and its celebration may amount to the crime of bigamy (Offences Against the Person Act 1861, s.57). A person can validly remarry only after the death of a former spouse (see below on the problem of missing spouses) or after a valid decree of divorce or, where the marriage is voidable, nullity.

Not all bigamous marriages will amount to the crime of bigamy. Prosecutions are generally brought only where the bigamous partner deceived the other. In addition there are a number of defences to the crime of bigamy, in particular that the bigamous partner believed in good faith and on reasonable grounds that his or her first spouse was dead or that the marriage had been dissolved or annulled (*R.* v. *Tolson* (1889); *R.* v. *Gould* (1968)). In both these cases the marriage will still be void if the first spouse is in fact alive and the marriage still subsists but there will be no criminal conviction for bigamy.

In addition, if the accused's first spouse had been missing continuously for at least seven years and he or she had no knowledge that the spouse was alive at the time of the second marriage ceremony this will be a good defence to a charge of bigamy. If the missing spouse subsequently turns up alive, however, the marriage will be void. Protection against this contingency is provided by asking for a decree of presumption of death and dissolution of marriage (Matrimonial Causes Act 1973, s.19). This is a decree of divorce made on the basis that the missing spouse is dead. The petitioner must satisfy the court "that reasonable grounds exist for supposing that the other party to the marriage is dead" and, for this purpose, death is presumed if the spouse has been absent for an uninterrupted period of at least seven years in circumstances in which the petitioner has no reason to believe that his spouse was alive. Absence for a shorter period than seven years raises no such presumption but it will, of course, still be possible to bring forward other evidence which will lead the court to presume death. If the first spouse turns up alive *after* the decree has been pronounced any second marriage remains valid, the decree being one of divorce.

3. Formalities of marriage

The actual formalities required for the solemnisation of a marriage in England depend on whether it is celebrated according to the rites of the Church of England or on the authority of a superintendent registrar's certificate (in which case the ceremony may be either civil or celebrated according to the rites of some other sect or religion). The necessary formalities are laid down in the Marriage Acts 1949–1970.

First, however, the matter of parental consent must be considered.

(a) *Parental consent*

Anyone between the ages of 16–18, except a widow or widower, is required to obtain their parents' consent to their marriage. It must be stressed, however, that failure to obtain that consent does *not* render the marriage void if the partners somehow manage to go through a valid ceremony without it. The marriage will remain valid but the spouses will probably have committed some criminal offence and be liable to prosecution. The offence may be forgery or making a false statement, for example.

Parents may, of course, be dead or divorced. The precise list of persons whose consent is required and in what circumstances is given in the Marriage Act 1949, Sched. 2:

(i) *Where the Bride or Bridegroom is Legitimate*

Circumstances	Person(s) whose consent is required
Where both parents are living:	
(a) if both parents are living together;	Both parents.
(b) if parents are divorced or separated by court order or by agreement;	The parent to whom custody is committed by court order or by agreement, or if custody is shared, both parents.
(c) if one parent has been deserted by the other;	The parent who has been deserted.
(d) if both parents have been deprived of custody by order of any court.	The person to whom custody is committed by order of the court.
Where one parent is dead:	
(a) if there is no other guardian;	The surviving parent.
(b) if a guardian has been appointed by the deceased parent.	The surviving parent and the guardian if acting jointly, or the surviving parent or the guardian if the parent or guardian is sole guardian.

| Where both parents are dead. | The guardian or guardians appointed by the deceased parents or by a court. |

(ii) *Where the Bride or Bridegroom is Illegitimate*

| If the mother is alive. | The mother or, if she has been deprived of custody by a court, the person to whom custody has been committed by the court. |
| If the mother is dead. | The guardian appointed by the mother. |

If the person between 16–18 is in care, either under a care order or as a result of a parental rights resolution (see *post*, p.135), it may be that the consent to the marriage of the local authority is required. This matter is not dealt with in Schedule 2 and is not clear.

If a parent will not consent, is unobtainable or is incapable of consenting because of disability, then an application may be made to the High Court, county court or magistrates' court. The usual forum is the magistrates' court which sits as a domestic court from which the public are excluded and where publicity is restricted. Notice of the application must be served on any party refusing consent. There is no appeal from the courts' decision. It is not known what principles, if any, the courts use in deciding whether to give or refuse consent to marriage.

(b) *Marriage in the Church of England*
There is a choice of four preliminaries to a Church of England marriage ceremony:

(i) The publication of banns of matrimony. This consists of an announcement of a proposed marriage during service in church on three Sundays. It is made to the congregation by a clergyman in the following words prescribed by the Book of Common Prayer: "I publish the banns of marriage between . . . of . . . and . . . of . . . If any of you know cause or just impediment, why these two persons should not be joined together in holy matrimony ye are to declare it. This is the first/second/third time of asking." Banns may have to be published in more than one church according to the residential qualifications of the bride and bridegroom or the choice by either of them of their "usual place of worship" for the wedding ceremony.

(ii) The grant of a common licence. This is granted by a diocesan bishop acting through his chancellor. It enables the marriage to take place in a church or chapel in whose parish or district either party has resided for 15 days immediately before the grant, or in the usual place of worship of either of them. Before a licence is granted either the bride or bridegroom must swear to the truth of specified particulars indicating that there is no obstacle to the proposed marriage. A licence is not granted if a *caveat* has been entered against a grant unless the *caveat* is withdrawn or an ecclesiastical judge has after investigation ruled against it.

(iii) The issue of a superintendent registrar's certificate. Such a certificate authorises the solemnisation of a marriage in any church or chapel where banns would have had to be published, provided the minister or another clergyman agrees to officiate. The procedure leading to the issue of a certificate begins with "notice of marriage" to the superintendent registrar of the district where each party has resided for at least seven days prior to giving notice. At the time of giving notice a "solemn declaration" that no obstacle to the proposed marriage exists is required. The notice is then entered in "the marriage notice book" which is open to the public without charge, and exhibited in some conspicuous place in the registrar's office for 21 successive days. Unless a *caveat* is entered, a certificate is issued after completion of this procedure. The Registrar General, if necessary, adjudicates on the validity of a *caveat*.

(iv) The issue of a special licence. Such a licence is granted on special application to the Archbishop of Canterbury acting through the Faculty Officer. It enables a wedding to take place anywhere and without any delay.

The actual ceremony must take place within three months of the appropriate preliminaries between the hours of 8 a.m. and 6 p.m. at the church where banns were called or named in the licence or certificate. There must be two witnesses apart from the officiating clergyman.

(c) *Marriage under a Superintendent Registrar's Certificate*

All ceremonies of marriage which are not performed in accordance with the rites of the Church of England are preceded by a superintendent registrar's certificate which may be issued "without licence" or "by licence." Both forms of certificate require as preliminary procedure the giving of notice to one or more superintendent registrars, according to circumstances, and the making of a solemn declaration that there is no known impediment to the proposed marriage. The advantage of a certificate of licence is that only one of the parties needs to give notice and, unless a *caveat* has been entered or the issue of a certificate has been forbidden, the wedding can take place without the compulsory delay one clear day after notice.

The ceremony may take place in any "registered building"—normally a place of religious worship registered for the solemnisation of marriages by the Registrar General. Alternatively it may take place according to a civil ceremony in the office of the superintendent registrar (register office). In both cases, whatever form of ceremony is adopted, at some point each partner must make a declaration that he or she knows of no impediment to the marriage and takes the other as his/her wedded wife or husband

(d) *Defective formalities*

As we have seen, non-compliance with one formality—the need for parental consent—does not render the marriage void. The same is true of non-compliance with a number of other formalities. A marriage will be void for defective formalities only if those specified in sections 25 and 49 of the Marriage Act 1949 are "knowingly and wilfully" not complied with. Broadly the crucial formalities are those relating to the validity of the preliminaries (*i.e.* the licence or certificate) or where the marriage takes place in the wrong place or before the wrong celebrant. A marriage is presumed valid unless the evidence shows beyond reasonable doubt that both parties knew at the time of the ceremony that one of the relevant formalities was not being complied with (*Mahadervan* (1964)).

(e) *Possible reforms*

It can be seen from the above that there are a number of possible ways of getting married and no clear purpose is achieved by this plethora of methods. As long ago as 1971 the Law Commission (Report No. 53, 1971) recommended change. They considered that the aim of a sound marriage law should be to ensure that only those free to marry can get a marriage solemnised and that there should be adequate safeguards against secret marriages. Accordingly they recommend a uniform civil procedure as a preliminary to all marriages involving a 15 day waiting period between the giving of notice and receiving authorisation to marry. Common licences should be abolished. The parties should be required to state the date and place of their birth to guard marriages being solemnised without a necessary parental consent. The Commission also recommend the abolition of banns, which would incidentally have the virtue of abolishing a considerable body of complicated case law concerning the validity of banns called in false names (see *Chipchase* (1942); *Small* (1923)). None of these proposals have yet been embodied in legislation.

4. Living together as husband and wife

What is the legal position of a man and woman who live together without marrying? If they live together as husband and wife the relationship is often referred to as a "common law" marriage. This concept, however, is not recognised by English law—a person is either validly married or not and a valid marriage can only be created by a valid marriage ceremony. However, increasingly, the law has had to recognise that it would be unfair to treat a cohabiting couple as though they were "strangers" to each other and some of both the benefits and burdens of matrimony have been extended to them. It is not proposed to give an exhaustive account of the law affecting cohabitants at this point but throughout this book wherever a "matrimonial" remedy is discussed the question of whether it is also applicable to cohabiting couples will be noted. A number of examples illustrate how cohabiting couples are now being treated in a similar manner to married couples by the law. A cohabitant has been treated as a member of her partner's "family" for the purposes of succeeding to his Rent Act tenancy after his death (*Dyson* v. *Fox* (1975)). A cohabitant has been given similar rights to succeed to a secure council house tenancy on the death of the tenant partner (Housing Act 1980). Cohabitants are treated in the same way as married couples for the purposes of the Housing (Homeless Persons) Act 1977 and in relation to rent rebates and allowances under the Housing Finance Act 1972.

Cohabitants are given similar rights as are given to married couples to obtain injunctions against molestation and to exclude the other partner from the home under the Domestic Violence and Matrimonial Proceedings Act 1976. A dependent cohabitant can apply for provision from the estate of his or her partner under the Inheritance (Provision for Family and Dependants) Act 1975. The courts will tend to treat cohabitants in much the same way as spouses where there is a dispute relating to the ownership of the matrimonial home (see *Cooke* v. *Head* (1972); *Eves* v. *Eves* (1975)). The DHSS will treat married couples and cohabitants in the same way when deciding entitlement to supplementary benefit or family income supplement.

However, there remain important differences between the married and the unmarried. Obviously none of the legislation designed to deal with matrimonial disputes applies to cohabitants. A cohabitant cannot therefore apply for maintenance or a property adjustment order, nor does a cohabitant benefit from the provisions of the Matrimonial Homes Act 1967. A cohabitant has no claim for compensation under the Fatal Accidents Act. The Inland Revenue will not treat a cohabiting couple as though they were married (this is often advantageous to cohabiting couples however). Finally, the children of cohabiting couples are categorised as illegitimate and different rules apply to them in relation to maintenance, custody, inheritance and nationality.

Thus there remain many legal provisions which regulate husbands and wives but do not extend to informal liaisons, and this often leaves the unmarried couple, especially the woman with children, at a disadvantage. Could an unmarried couple make a legally enforceable "cohabitation contract" in order to avoid some of these disadvantages? Such contracts have been much discussed recently but not yet tested in the courts. They might be considered contrary to public policy, as are contracts by married couples to regulate a future separation, or any other contract prejudicial to marriage or contrary to morality. There would seem to be nothing prejudicial to public policy in agreements designed to regulate some of the incidents of living together, such as the ownership of the house or other property, provided that cohabitation was not used as the consideration for such agreements (see for example the facts in *Tanner* v. *Tanner* (1975)). The courts would not enforce any terms which attempted to regulate the custody of or access to children (see further p.107 on this).

5. Recognition of foreign marriages

In general a marriage validly celebrated abroad will be recognised as valid in England. In the past, however, English courts have found great difficulty in dealing with one type of foreign marriage, the polygamous marriage. How far should such a marriage be recognised as valid by the English courts? Polygamous marriages certainly did not comply with the classic definition of marriage laid down in *Hyde* (1866), that marriage is the "union for life of *one* man and *one* woman, to the exclusion of all others." To fail to recognise polygamous marriages at all would have resulted in the offspring of such unions being regarded as illegitimate in England, and permit the "spouses" to marry in England as though the polygamous union had not taken place. The courts did not adopt this line of thinking (in *Bamgbose* v. *Daniel* (1955) and *Baindail* (1946)). They considered that matrimonial relief in England was geared to the monogamous union and that therefore a polygamously married person could not avail himself of the matrimonial remedies provided in England. This also applied to a person whose marriage was merely potentially polygamous, in that although he could take another wife, he only had one at the time of the dispute.

This rule caused hardship, especially with the influx of Commonwealth immigrants after 1945, many of whose marriages were at least potentially polygamous. The Law Commission therefore recommended that matrimonial relief should be granted to polygamously married couples and this has now been enacted in the Matrimonial Proceedings (Polygamous Marriages) Act 1972. The courts may now grant matrimonial relief, such as divorce, nullity, judicial separation, maintenance and orders in relation to property even where the petitioner is polygamously married to the respondent and actually has another spouse living.

It may be wondered if, where a man validly marries two wives in a country which permits polygamy and then comes to live in England, one of those wives could petition for a divorce in England alleging his adultery with the other wife. This petition would not succeed, for, as the Law Commission pointed out (Report No. 42, Polygamous Marriages, p.18), sexual intercourse with one's spouse cannot amount to adultery in English law.

This Act does not alter the law that the only type of marriage that can be validly contracted in England is a monogamous marriage, even where the law of the spouse's domicile permits him to contract a polygamous marriage. Nor can a person domiciled in England contract such a marriage abroad—such a marriage will be void (Matrimonial Proceedings (Polygamous Marriages) Act 1972, s.3). Thus many immigrants now domiciled in England cannot contract a valid polygamous marriage even though their religion may permit it, and even if they go back, temporarily, to their country of origin to contract such a marriage. This would apply even though such a marriage was only potentially polygamous.

One situation is still not entirely clear. Suppose a woman domiciled in England goes to Egypt and contracts a polygamous marriage with a man domiciled in Egypt. Is the validity of the marriage determined by the woman's *ante* nuptial domicile (England) or her intended *post* nuptial domicile (Egypt)? Opinions differ on this and there are no conclusive cases. In *Radwan* (1972) the court favoured basing their decision on the *post* nuptial domicile but the *ante* nuptial domicile was favoured in *Padolecchia* (1968).

For the purpose of claiming social security benefits, a polygamous marriage will only be recognised as valid for as long as it is in fact monogamous (Social Security Act 1975, s.162 (*b*)). However, a husband will be liable to contribute towards the maintenance of his wife where she is receiving supplementary benefit even if the marriage is polygamous in fact as well as in law (*Din* v. *N.A.B.* (1967)).

A note on domicile

The concept of domicile can be very important as a person's status—married, divorced, adopted, legitimate, illegitimate, etc.—can depend upon his or her domicile.

According to English law nobody is ever without a domicile and, in general, a person is domiciled in the country where he has his permanent home, whether or not he happens to be a national of that country. "Domicile" and "nationality" therefore often coincide, but they are not necessarily the same and a change of nationality does not automatically result in a change of domicile or vice versa. A feature peculiar to the notion of domicile is that one can be domiciled only in a country with its own legal system. If Edinburgh is, therefore, somebody's permanent home his domicile is Scottish, not British or United Kingdom, as the Scots have their own legal system. Similarly, a person residing permanently in the state of California, which equally has its own laws, is domiciled in that state and not in the United States of America. Conversely a person who has his permanent home in Wales has an English domicile, as Wales has no legal system of its own, and is governed by the laws of England.

Every person is deemed at birth to possess a "domicile of origin." The domicile of origin of a legitimate child born during his father's lifetime is that of its father at the time of the child's birth. The domicile of a child born after its father's death, or of an illegitimate child, is that of its mother at the time of the child's birth. A child's domicile at birth, therefore, depends on that of his father or mother, as the case may be, and the child's domicile continues to be dependent on that of its father or mother until the age of 16 (Domicile and Matrimonial Proceedings Act 1973, s.3). After the age of 16 a person acquires an independent domicile. The domicile of a married woman throughout the duration of a marriage used to be that of her husband, and therefore changed whenever his changed. Now the Domicile and Matrimonial Proceedings Act 1973, s.1, abolishes this dependent domicile of a wife. Her domicile is now determined in the same way as that of any other independent person.

An adult may acquire a "domicile of choice." This is done by leaving the country of one's domicile of origin and taking up residence in another country with a settled intention of living there permanently. Given this intention, a "domicile of choice" is acquired on arrival and lost on departure if the intention has been abandoned (*Re Flynn decd.* (1968)). The loss of domicile of choice automatically results in the revival of the "domicile of origin" which lasts until another "domicile of choice"is acquired at a future date.

CHAPTER 2

HUSBAND AND WIFE

What are the legal consequences of marriage? Most of the law
relating to husband and wife has evolved from the need to resolve
disputes between spouses when the marriage breaks down—on
divorce or separation. The law is not much concerned with
marriages which are going concerns. Other aspects of the law on
husband and wife have grown up as a result of the intervention or
interest of a third party, *e.g.* a mortgagee, the Inland Revenue, a
creditor or the social security authorities. In this chapter we are
concerned mainly with the legal rules that govern the position of
husbands and wives and their relationships with third parties whilst
the marriage subsists. We are also concerned with the situation
where one of the spouses dies. The rules and remedies that govern
the situation when the marriage breaks down are dealt with in Part
II of this book.

1. The duty to cohabit

To most people marriage involves living together, enjoying each
other's company and having a sexual relationship. Married couples
are said to have a legal right to "consortium." But this legal right is
incapable of precise definition; no one element—a common home,
affection, a sexual relationship—is essential. Consortium is "a
bundle of rights hardly capable of precise definition"; it is
"essentially an abstraction" (*Best* v. *Samuel Fox Ltd.* (1952)). This
lack of definition does not really matter very much as the right to
consortium is not directly enforceable. The old action for "restitution of conjugal rights" has now been abolished (Matrimonial
Proceedings and Property Act 1970, s.20). Disobedience to a decree
of restitution could, at one time, result in imprisonment or
excommunication from the Church of England, penalties which
were abolished in 1884 and 1813 respectively. Neither spouse has
the right to "force" the other to live with them. In *R.* v. *Jackson*
(1891) Mrs. Jackson was dragged from her carriage by Mr. Jackson
and an accomplice and imprisoned in her husband's house. A
relative successfully applied for the writ of habeas corpus to release
her and so finally established that a husband did not have any right
physically to confine his wife.

A husband used to be able to protect his right to his wife's
consortium by a variety of actions which have now been abolished
by the Law Reform (Miscellaneous Provisions) Act 1970, ss. 4 and

5. He can no longer claim damages from a stranger for "harbour-ing" or "enticing" his wife, nor can he sue a co-respondent for damages for adultery.

The concept of consortium is therefore of little practical relevance nowadays. Breach of the duty will generally constitute desertion and therefore provide a basis for divorce or some other matrimonial relief (see p.68). There also remains the anachronistic action whereby a husband may sue a person, in tort or for breach of contract, for damages for the loss of his wife's consortium. The basis for this action is not so much loss of consortium as loss of a wife's services. A husband is regarded as having a right to his wife's (and his minor children's) services and can sue someone who unlawfully deprives him of them; for example, someone who negligently injures her. Damages can cover any financial loss resulting from his wife's inability to perform domestic services, loss of her earnings and the cost of medical and other treatment (*Kirkham* v. *Boughey* (1958)). If the wife dies then a claim must be made under the Fatal Accidents Act (see p.37).

A wife does not have a reciprocal right to damages for loss of her husband's consortium or services. In *Best* v. *Samuel Fox Ltd.* (1952) an attempt was made to establish equality between husband and wife by making a claim on behalf of a wife for the impairment of her husband's consortium consisting of his permanent incapacity for sexual intercourse due to injuries which he received in an accident for which the defendants were legally responsible. On the wife's behalf it was argued that it was anomalous in modern times to deny to a wife a legal remedy which in identical circumstances was open to a husband. The answer of the House of Lords was that the real anomaly was the husband's cause of action and they accordingly refused to extend it by giving a wife a reciprocal right.

The right to sue for the loss of a wife's or child's services will be abolished when the Administration of Justice Bill 1982, clause 2 is passed and becomes effective. The Bill was introduced in the House of Lords in February 1982.

2. Maintenance

At common law a husband is under a duty to maintain his wife but she owes no similar duty to him. The origin of the rule is the doctrine of unity of husband and wife, as expressed by Blackstone on his *Commentaries* (1765):

> "By marriage, the husband and wife are one person in law; that is, the very being or legal existence of the woman is suspended during the marriage, or at least is incorporated and consoli-

dated with that of the husband under whose wing, protection and cover she performs everything."

This doctrine meant that nearly all a wife's property passed to her husband on marriage and she, being incapable of ownership and therefore of contracting, was thus totally dependent on him. The common law did not, however, provide an effective means whereby a wife could *enforce* her right to be maintained even though it made elaborate provision concerning the termination of the duty. A wife who deserted her husband or committed adultery lost her common law right to be maintained.

The common law right or duty has now little, if any, relevance because it has been superseded by statutory provisions which, in certain circumstances, require both spouses to maintain each other. Most of these provisions relate to the breakdown of marriage, either on divorce, where a separated wife makes an application for supplementary benefit (see *post*, p.32), on nullity, or on separation. How far is the duty to maintain enforceable whilst the marriage is still subsisting and the parties living together? The basic rule is still that it is not enforceable. A wife (or husband) has no automatic right to a proportion of the other's income. Even where a housekeeping allowance is given the donor remains the owner of the allowance (but see *post*, p.29 for the position relating to *savings* from housekeeping money). Where the husband receives a social security benefit which includes an amount for his wife the full amount will be paid to him and the wife will find it very difficult to do anything effective about it if he does not pay over the money to her. There are two possibilities open to a wife who wishes to try to enforce her right to maintenance whilst continuing to live with her husband:

(a) *Wife's right to pledge her husband's credit*

The only way under the old common law whereby a wife could make her right to maintenance effective was to pledge her husband's credit for "necessaries." This meant that the husband was liable to pay any debts she incurred in providing herself with "things that are really necessary and suitable to the style in which the husband chooses to live." This right, known as the agency of necessity, was abolished by the Matrimonial Proceedings and Property Act 1970, s.41.

However, it is still possible for a wife to pledge her husband's credit in connection with what is sometimes known as the "common household agency." A wife living with her husband and managing his household is presumed to have his authority to pledge his credit for necessary household purchases. He will then be liable for the bills. The husband can avoid this liability if he can show that he had forbidden his wife to pledge his credit or that he was giving her an adequate allowance. However, a tradesman who has supplied the wife on credit in the past will be entitled to assume that the wife's authority continues until notified by the husband of its revocation.

This household agency is not confined to spouses. A housekeeper or cohabitant who manages another's household will also be entitled to act as a "common household agent."

(b) *Application for maintenance*

A spouse can apply to the magistrates' court for maintenance even though still living with the other (see section 25 of the Domestic Proceedings and Magistrates' Courts Act 1978). The applicant must establish one of the grounds in section 1, which includes simply "neglect to maintain" (see further on the grounds p.55). An order for maintenance can be made whilst the parties are living together but it will be enforceable for only six months. The Act says nothing about the enforceability of an order for the payment of a lump sum made when the parties are living together.

3. Matrimonial property

Marriage as such does not affect the *ownership* of property though it does affect the right to *occupy* the matrimonial home. There is, therefore, little *matrimonial* property law because in general the ordinary law applies. Each spouse retains his or her own property on marriage and also owns whatever he or she acquires after it. Cohabitants are therefore treated in much the same way as spouses in this context.

It is frequently difficult to decide who "owns" any items of property as few couples keep their earnings and other resources rigidly separated. Property is often acquired in joint names, from joint savings or by one partner with help from the other. At the time of acquisition neither party generally gives much thought to legal ownership or what should happen if they should cease to live together. Disputes arise on divorce or separation. When a couple got divorced before 1971 it was vital to know who owned what because the courts had no power to order one party to transfer property to the other. An order for payment of periodic maintenance or for the payment of a lump sum could be made, but the court could not order one spouse to transfer a specific item of property, *e.g.* the house, to the other. Often legal title to the home was in the name of the husband alone. A wife could claim a share in it only if she could show, under the normal rules relating to real property, that she had acquired an interest in it. This was generally done by showing that the husband held the property on trust for them both as beneficial owners.

Nowadays it is not so vital for a wife to prove that she has some legally recognised interest in the property because the court can give her a share of it on divorce or judicial separation by using their powers under section 24 of the Matrimonial Causes Act 1973 (see p.87). Nevertheless it is often still important to know who owns what. First, on divorce a wife is more likely to get a decent share in any property if she can show that in fact she already has a legal or equitable interest in it. Secondly, it will be important to know who owns what on the death of either spouse and also wherever there is a dispute with a third party such as a building society, trustee in bankruptcy or tax inspector. Thirdly, once divorced spouses have remarried they can no longer use sections 23 and 24 of the 1973 Act and any remaining disputes over property have to be settled according to the ordinary law. Finally, cohabitees are entirely unable to use the Matrimonial Causes Act, of course, and any disputes between them will be dealt with according to the rules described here, with some exceptions.

(a) Procedure in property disputes

The historical development of the law of property between spouses has been influenced by the informal and flexible procedure used to resolve disputes. Disputes between husband and wife regarding the "title to or possession of property" are generally resolved in proceedings brought under section 17 of the Married Women's Property Act 1882 in either the county or High Court. Section 17 allows the judge to "make such order with respect to the property in dispute . . . as he shall think fit." It is now established, however, that this wide power does *not* confer "jurisdiction to transfer any proprietary interest in property from one spouse to the other or to create new proprietary rights in either spouse" (*per* Lord Diplock in *Pettitt* (1970)). What the section does confer is a wide discretion concerning the *enforcement* of existing proprietary or possessory rights. In deciding, for example, whether to order the sale of a jointly owned home the court will consider the interests of the family as a whole and especially the needs of the children. It will follow similar principles as would be invoked if the issue arose on divorce under section 24 of the Matrimonial Causes Act 1973.

In this context it is interesting to note that although cohabitants cannot avail themselves of the Married Women's Property Act 1882, s.17, in cases where there is a dispute about the joint ownership and sale of a home, the court will probably follow similar principles in deciding whether or not to order a sale. The issue would be decided under the Law of Property Act 1925, s.30, and in *Re Evers Trust* (1980) Ormrod L. J. considered that in disputes relating to "family" property the court should adopt the same approach whether or not the couple were married. In this case an unmarried couple had jointly purchased a cottage for themselves and the woman's children to live in. The court refused to order a sale when the man left, on the basis that it was still needed as a home for the woman and her children.

Amendments to section 17 of the 1882 Act have widened its scope. Where the property subject to dispute has been disposed of at the time of the hearing the court can order the defendant to pay to the plaintiff a sum of money equivalent to his or her interest in the property or to make an order in respect of other property which represents the whole or part of the property in dispute (Matrimonial Causes (Property and Maintenance) Act 1958, s.7). Proceedings under section 17 can be begun at any time during the marriage or within three years of its dissolution or annulment (Matrimonial Proceedings and Property Act 1970, s.39).

(b) *The matrimonial home*

(i) Ownership. The principles determining the ownership of the matrimonial home are not wholly clear. This is due partly to the informality and lack of legal precision which is peculiar to domestic transactions and partly to the refusal of the House of Lords "to consider whether property belonging to either spouse ought to be regarded as family property, for that would be introducing a new concept into English law and not merely developing existing principles" (*Pettitt* (1970) *per* Lord Reid). The Law Commission has produced a Report (No.86, 1978) in which they recommend that the matrimonial home should be jointly owned. No legislation to bring this into effect has been introduced. In the meantime, as has already been mentioned, the unsatisfactory state of the law is likely to be less serious in practice as the great majority of disputes between parties to a marriage about the ownership of the matrimonial home occur only if a marriage breaks up, and the courts now have wide powers to adjust and transfer the ownership of any property belonging to a married person on the grant of a decree of divorce, nullity or judicial separation.

Subject to the possibility of adjustment, the general approach to the ownership of the matrimonial home is that, where there is evidence of an agreement about ownership between the parties to a marriage, the agreement is conclusive. In the absence of agreement, the respective proprietary interests of the parties depend on their inferred intention or, possibly, on what would amount to a just division of the property.

The legal techniques used to give effect to the above approach are the implied, resulting and constructive trust, or a mixture of them. An implied trust arises where it can be inferred from the parties' conduct that they intended to hold property jointly. A resulting trust can arise where one person puts property into the name of another. In the absence of an intention to make an out and out gift the donee will hold the property on trust for the donor. The property "results back" to the donor. A constructive trust arises from the conduct of the parties and the way property is managed or dealt with, irrespective of any intention, express or implied, of the parties.

The cases in which the court is faced with the task of inferring the intention of the parties concerning the ownership of the matrimonial home fall into two broad categories. The first comprises those cases in which only one of the parties contributed to its acquisition. In this type of case if the only name on the legal title to the home is that of the spouse who contributed all the purchase money, then he or she is the sole owner of the home and the other has no proprietary interest of any kind. However, if the spouse who provides the purchase money puts the home in the name of the other spouse, or of both of them, then the other spouse may have a beneficial interest, depending on how far this was the intention of the contributing spouse. A summary of the position was made by Lord Upjohn in *Pettitt's* case:

> "In the absence of *all* evidence, if a husband puts property into his wife's name he intends it to be a gift to her but if he puts it into joint names then (in the absence of all other evidence) the presumption is the same as a joint beneficial tenancy. If a wife puts property into her husband's name it may be that in the absence of all other evidence he is a trustee for her but in practice there will in almost every case be some explanation (however slight) of this (today) rather unusual course. If a wife puts property into their joint names I would think that a joint beneficial tenancy was intended, for I can see no other reason for it."

The second category includes all cases in which both parties have made a direct financial contribution to the acquisition of the matrimonial home. In these cases the beneficial ownership is shared between the parties whether the legal title to the property is in their joint names or in the name of only one of them; and their respective shares are equal unless the evidence of their conduct establishes a clear intention of sharing ownership in definite unequal proportions. The outcome of equal ownership, in the absence of rebutting evidence in this type of case, was justified by Lord Denning in *Rimmer's* case (1953) as follows:

"It seems to me that when the parties, by their joint efforts, save money to buy a house, which is intended as a continuing provision by them both, then the proper presumption is that the beneficial interest belongs to them both jointly. The property may be bought in the name of the husband alone or in the name of the wife alone, but nevertheless if it is bought with money saved by their joint efforts, and it is impossible fairly to distinguish between the efforts of the one and the other, then the beneficial interest should be presumed to belong to them both jointly".

The case of *Chapman* (1969) provides an illustration of this approach. The husband paid £680 and the wife £120 of the deposit on a home. The rest of the purchase price was raised by a mortgage for which the husband was responsible. The wife paid all housekeeping expenses from her earnings. When the marriage broke up the home was sold and a dispute arose over the division of the proceeds of sale (after the mortgage had been paid off). The court held that the spouses had put their joint resources into the purchase of the house and had made no clear agreement as to the shares each should own, and therefore the money should be divided equally between them, even though the wife's initial contribution was less than the husband's.

Given that where a spouse makes a contribution to the purchase of the home, he or she will, subject to a contrary intention, acquire a beneficial interest in it, the question that then arises is what amounts to a contribution. Clearly a direct money contribution will give such an interest. So also will an indirect finanical contribution, as where a wife uses her money for housekeeping so that the husband can use his to pay off the mortgage. However, this kind of contribution must be reasonably substantial to give rise to a beneficial interest. In *Tulley* (1965) the wife used her wages of £4 a week for housekeeping purposes, thus enabling her husband to devote his money to paying off the mortgage. It was held that this was not enough to give her an interest in the home and it belonged solely to the husband. If an indirect contribution is substantial enough then it will give a spouse an interest in the home and there is no need to establish any agreement between the spouses that the house should be jointly owned (*Hazell* (1972)).

Where a spouse's contribution take the form of work then there are two situations in which he or she might get an interest in a home purchased by the other. First, where a spouse does unpaid work which would normally be paid, as in *Nixon* (1969) where the house was bought by the husband largely with the profits from his market stall which the wife had helped to run without receiving any wages. She was held to have a half interest in the home. However, where a wife discharges the "normal" functions of housewife and mother she gains no interest in the home purchased by her husband as the courts do not regard this work as work which normally would be paid for as in *Nixon* (see *Pettitt* (1970), at p.794). Secondly, if a spouse makes improvements to the home he or she may get an interest in it. This is a statutory rule under section 37 of the Matrimonial Proceedings and Property Act 1970:

> Where a husband or wife contributes in money or money's worth to the improvement of . . . property in which or in the proceeds of sale of which either or both of them has or have a beneficial interest, the husband or wife so contributing shall, if the contribution is of a substantial nature and subject to any agreement between them to the contrary . . . be treated as having then acquired by virtue of his or her contribution a share or an enlarged share, as the case may be, in that beneficial interest of such an extent as may have been then agreed, or, in default of such agreement, as may seem in all the circumstances just to any court before which the question of the existence or extent of the beneficial interest of the husband or wife arises.

It must be noted that the contribution must be substantial. *Pettitt* (1970) would probably be decided the same way today as three of their Lordships considered that the improvements made by the husband to the home—decorating and woodwork—were of an ephemeral nature and were the kind of household tasks that husbands normally undertook.

These rules apply not only to husbands and wives but can also apply to cohabitants. For example in *Cooke* v. *Head* (1972) the home was legally owned by the man but his cohabitant paid some of the expenses and also did a considerable amount of building work on the house. She was awarded a one third interest in the home. (See also *Richards* v. *Dove* (1974) and *Eves* (1975)). Another line of argument was used in the case of *Pascoe* v. *Turner* (1979). Mr. Turner and Mrs. Pascoe lived as man and wife but when Mr. Turner eventually left for another he promised Mrs. Pascoe that the house and everything in it was hers. Mrs. Pascoe spent money on the house. Mr. Turner was estopped from denying the gift and ordered by the Court of Appeal to transfer the house to Mrs. Pascoe.

(ii) Occupation. When a marriage breaks down, the right to occupy the matrimonial home is as important as its ownership. Can either party evict the other? Is the spouse who has no beneficial interest in the home liable to be evicted by a third party such as a mortgagee, landlord or purchaser? The answers to these questions differ according to whether only one of the parties or both have beneficial interests in the matrimonial home.

(a) *Owner occupiers*
(i) In cases where one party is entitled to a legal or equitable interest in the home, the position of the other is protected by the Matrimonial Homes Act 1967. By virtue of this Act the party without a legal interest in the matrimonial home is automatically entitled to what are called "rights of occupation." These consist of the right not to be evicted or excluded from the matrimonial home by the other party except with the leave of the court and (should the protected party be out of occupation) the right to enter and occupy the house with the leave of the court.

These "rights of occupation" cease on the termination of the marriage unless an application has been made to a court beforehand and the court has extended the rights for a specified period or until further order. The court may declare, enforce, restrict, terminate or regulate the exercise of the rights of occupation conferred by the Act or of any other rights of occupation (see Domestic Violence and Matrimonial Proceedings Act 1976, s.3). Amongst its wide powers the court "may except part of the dwelling house from a spouse's right of occupation" and further "may impose on either spouse obligations as to the repair and maintenance of the dwelling house or the discharge of any liabilities in respect of it." In exercising its powers "the court may make such order as it thinks just and reasonable having regard to the conduct of the spouses in relation to each other and otherwise to their respective needs and financial resources, to the needs of any children and to all the circumstances of the case." The High Court and the county court have equal jurisdiction over all matters arising under this Act.

The need for protection of the spouse without any beneficial interest in the matrimonial home against a third party arose after the judgment of the House of Lords in the case of *National Provincial Bank* v. *Ainsworth* (1965). It was decided that a deserted wife without a beneficial interest was liable to be evicted from the matrimonial home by a bona fide purchaser from her husband or the mortgagee of the premises even though they knew of her presence and the fact that she was a deserted wife. The Matrimonial Homes Act 1967 (ss. 3–6) aims to nullify the effect of this case by providing a method which makes "the rights of occupation" created by the Act binding on third parties. Such a right becomes a charge on the other party's estate or interest so that it can be registered as a land charge or, in the case of the registered land, be protected by a notice. The purpose of this device is to give the protected spouse's rights of occupation priority over a purchaser or mortgagee. However, this protection will operate only where the spouse's rights of occupation under the Act arose and was registered *before* the sale, mortgage or other dealing with the property. The rights of occupation do not bind a trustee in bankruptcy if the owner spouse has become insolvent.

In cases where a mortgage was created by the owner spouse before the other spouse's right of occupation arose (as where a mortgage was taken out when the house was bought) then, if the mortgage payments fall into arrears, the Building Society may sue for possession of the house. The non-owning spouse is entitled to be told of these proceedings, be joined in the action and, if he or she can pay off the arrears, may succeed in preventing a possession order from being made (Matrimonial Homes and Property Act 1981, s.2).

(ii) Where both spouses have a beneficial interest in the matrimonial home there exists what is known as a trust for sale. This means that both parties, by virtue of their proprietary interests, have a right of occupation and, if necessary, may obtain an injunction against any attempt of eviction or exclusion by the other. They can also make an application under the Matrimonial Homes Act 1967. If there is a deadlock between them regarding the occupation or disposal of the home either may apply to the court for the enforcement of the trust by an order for sale. This will not be made if the marriage is still viable and a reconciliation possible (*Rawlings* (1964)) but, where the marriage has been terminated or is dead in fact, an order for sale may be made unless it is considered desirable to maintain the status quo pending matrimonial proceedings between the parties so that all ancillary questions can be determined at the same time (*Jones* v. *Challenger* (1961), *Bedson* (1965)). Even after a divorce a sale will not be ordered if the house is still needed to provide a home for the remaining spouse and the children. In ordering or refusing a sale the court should exercise its discretion in the same way as it would when making financial and property orders under the Matrimonial Causes Act 1973, ss. 23 and 24 (*Williams* (1977)).

A spouse with a beneficial interest in the matrimonial home will generally be able to protect his interest against third parties. If the property is in the joint names of husband and wife, then of course both must consent to any dealings with the home, so there can be no question of one spouse's rights being lost because of a surreptitious transaction by the other. On the other hand, if the legal title is in the name of only one of the parties, the other having a beneficial interest as described on p.22, then the other spouse would be wise to register his or her interest. The simplest way to do this is to register occupation rights under the Matrimonial Homes Act 1967, as already described (1967 Act, s.1(9)). However, a spouse's beneficial interest in the home will be protected against third parties even if the interest is *not* registered in any way, at least if the land is registered land. This is the effect of the House of Lords decision in *Williams & Glyn's Bank* v. *Boland and Brown* (1980). Mrs. Boland had contributed towards the purchase price of the matrimonial home but the title to it was in her husband's name alone and she had not registered her interest under either the Matrimonial Homes Act or under any other enactment. Mr. Boland mortgaged the house for business purposes to the bank, who made no effort to investigate the wife's position. When Mr. Boland failed to repay his loan the bank began possession proceedings. The court held that the wife's rights in the home took priority over the rights of the bank; they were an "overriding interest" under the Land Registration Act 1925, s.70(*g*). Her actual occupation of the home, coupled with her beneficial interest in it, meant that the bank should have investigated her position and was bound by her rights. It could not evict her in order to sell the house. It is generally thought that this decision will apply also to unregistered land, and that it could also apply where the couple were cohabiting and not married.

(b) *Tenants*

Where the home is rented and one spouse alone is the tenant, the other has rights to occupy it under the Matrimonial Homes Act 1967, as already described. If the tenancy is one to which the Rent Act 1977 or the Housing Act 1980 applies then the court has wide powers under the Matrimonial Homes Act 1967, s.7, to transfer the tenancy from one spouse to the other, or from their joint names to the name of only one of them. This may be done on granting a decree of divorce, judicial separation or nullity (see Matrimonial Homes and Property Act 1981, s.6). The landlord must be given an opportunity of being heard by the court before the order for transfer is made, but his consent to it is not required. There is also a power to transfer tenancies under section 24 of the Matrimonial Causes Act 1973 (*Thompson* (1976)). These powers apply to married couples only, not cohabitants. This means, for example, that if cohabitants are joint tenants of a council house and the woman leaves because of violence, there is no way that the court can transfer the tenancy to the woman even though she may have the children to look after. Neither can the council, as landlord, transfer the tenancy to her because the 1980 Housing Act gives council tenants security of

tenure and the council cannot therefore gain possession of the home
as against the man unless it succeeds in getting a possession order
under one of the grounds for possession specified in the Housing Act
1980. A woman in this situation may be able to get an injunction
excluding the man from the home under the Domestic Violence and
Matrimonial Proceedings Act 1976, but this will rarely last for
longer than three months and will not affect his property rights as
tenant (see *post*, p.47).

A most important protection for the wives of tenants of regulated
or controlled property is that even if the husband leaves the home
and tells the landlord that he does not wish to continue the tenancy,
the landlord cannot evict the wife. The husband is deemed to remain
in possession through his wife (and he cannot evict her owing to the
provisions of the Matrimonial Homes Act 1967, s.1) and thus she
retains the benefit of security of tenure provided by the Rent Act.
The wife may tender the rent to the landlord and he must accept it.
Once again, these provisions do not apply to cohabitants (*Colin
Smith Music* v. *Ridge* (1975)).

(c) *Injunctions*

The powers of the courts to issue injunctions or make orders
excluding a spouse or cohabitee from the home, other than under the
Matrimonial Homes Act 1967, are described *post* on p.45.

(d) *Money, bank accounts and housekeeping*

The basic rules that apply to the ownership of the home apply
equally to other property. Each spouse remains the owner of his or
her own earnings, bank accounts, savings or items bought with their
own money. However, most spouses pool their property in some way
or another and it is often impossible to decide who owns what.
Where a couple operate a joint bank account it will normally be
assumed that they intended to own the account jointly and equally.
The balance of the account will pass to the survivor on death.
Acquisitions from the account will normally be joint property (*Jones*
v. *Maynard* (1951)). The fact that the couple contributed to the
account in unequal shares will not usually be sufficient to upset the
assumption that it is owned in equal shares.

The mere existence of a joint account or fund on which both
husband and wife draw is not by itself evidence of the creation of a
common pool. In *Re Bishop's* case (1965), for example, the manner in
which the spouses operated a joint account and drew money from it
and spent it was inconsistent with the concept of a common pool and
the wife therefore failed to establish a right to sharing the ownership

of investments made with moneys from the joint account in her husband's name. (See also *Harrods Ltd.* v. *Tester* (1937).)

Where a husband gives a wife housekeeping money from which she makes savings then the Married Women's Property Act 1964 provides:

> If any question arises as to the right of a husband or wife to money derived from any allowance made by the husband for the expenses of the matrimonial home or for similar purposes, or to any property acquired out of such money, the money or property shall, in the absence of any agreement between them to the contrary, be treated as belonging to the husband and wife in equal shares.

If, therefore, there are savings from a wife's housekeeping allowance and their ownership is not specially agreed between husband and wife, half of the savings or property acquired out of the savings are presumed to be a gift to the wife. Previously, at common law, any savings wholly belonged to the husband (*Blackwell* (1943)).

This Act does *not* apply between cohabitants and also does not apply where wives make housekeeping allowances to husbands!

(e) *Gifts*

Where gifts are made to a spouse, they belong to that spouse if that is the intention of the donor. In *Samson's* case it was even held that wedding presents are not necessarily intended to be given to the spouses jointly:

> . . . the court is fully entitled . . . to draw the inference (which was drawn in this case) that money and gifts in kind originating from one side of the family were intended for the husband and those from the other side from friends of that party, were intended for the wife (*per* Lord Hodson).

Gifts from one spouse to the other can be legally abortive due to the general law relating to the validity of gifts. This requires the execution of a deed or at least of a written document in respect of an interest in land (Law of Property Act 1925, ss. 51(1), 53(1)(*b*), (*c*)) and the execution of a deed, or "delivery" to the donee at the time of its presentation, in respect of a chattel. *Cole's* case (1964) is an example of the difficulty of reconciling the technical rules of property law with the special relationship of a married couple, so that an intended gift is not frustrated as Mr. Cole's was. He had furnished a new matrimonial home and during his wife's rapturous tour of inspection told her: "It's all your's." For the following 16 years he and his wife lived happily in this home, both regarding the furniture as the wife's property. Then financial disaster struck and Mr. Cole was adjudicated bankrupt with the result that rival claims for the furniture were made by Mrs. Cole and Mr. Cole's trustee in bankruptcy. In the ensuing litigation the latter's claim was successful on the ground that there had been no effective delivery of the furniture from Mr. to Mrs. Cole and that the intended present of the furniture, being legally imperfect, was therefore invalid.

It is normally clear when a spouse intends to make a gift to the other, and the presumption of advancement will often assist a wife to prove that her husband intended to make her a gift. However, the courts are unwilling to allow a spouse both to give his cake away and yet eat it, as is illustrated by the case of *Tinker* (1970). The husband put the house in the name of his wife so that his creditors could not take it should his business fail. His marriage failed and he sought to show that he did not intend to benefit his wife by the gift, merely to defeat his creditors. It was held that the presumption of advancement prevailed and the house belonged to the wife.

4. Tax

Married couples are accorded special treatment in the tax system which can sometimes be to their advantage, sometimes to their disadvantage. It is in tax law that the old doctrine of the unity of husband and wife (see p.17) still has important consequences. In general the married couple is treated as a single tax unit and the husband is the person who must deal with the Inland Revenue, who is liable to pay the tax of both himself and his wife, and who receives any overpaid tax back from the Revenue. The Income and Corporation Taxes Act 1970, s.37, provides that the income of a married woman "be deemed for income tax purposes to be his income and not to be her income." Both husband and wife (assuming that both are in paid employment) are entitled to a tax free personal allowance (currently £1,565). A husband, in addition, is entitled to a married man's allowance of £880. A married couple therefore will pay less income tax than a cohabiting couple providing they are liable to basic tax (30 per cent.) only. However, they will find themselves liable to pay higher rates of tax sooner than if they were treated as separately taxable individuals because their incomes are aggregated.

If the combined taxable income of the married couple exceeds £12,801 then they are liable to pay higher rates of tax on the excess (the rates start at 40 per cent. and go up in 5 per cent. leaps to 60 per cent.). It is at this point, therefore, that a married couple may find it financially advantageous to forgo the benefits of the married man's allowance and ask to be taxed as separate individuals. They are entitled to be so treated if both request it under the Finance Act

1971, s.23. They will then be regarded as an unmarried couple for the purposes of liability for tax on their *earned* income. Where their *unearned*, or investment, income is concerned, aggregation cannot be avoided and husband and wife are not permitted to be taxed separately on this income. If their joint investment income exceeds £6,250 then, in addition to normal income tax, an additional tax, known as the investment income surcharge, is levied, currently at 15 per cent. A cohabiting couple can each receive £6,250 of investment income before either of them is liable for investment income surcharge.

A further advantage to unmarried couples concerns the tax relief available on mortgage interest payments (Finance Act 1972, s.75). The interest paid on a loan of up to £25,000 taken out for the purchase or improvement of the taxpayer's main residence is entitled to tax relief. A married couple's entitlement cannot exceed £25,000 as their loans are added together. A cohabiting couple are each entitled to relief of up to £25,000, making a possible £50,000 for both of them.

Similar rules govern exemption from capital gains tax. A husband and wife become liable to pay this tax, together, if they make "chargeable gains" (*i.e.* broadly profits made on selling property or disposing of it for consideration) of over £3,000 in any one year. Cohabitants can both claim a £3,000 exemption from capital gains tax. However, disposals of property *between* husband and wife are not subject to this tax, whereas those between cohabitants are. Similarly, transfers of property (*i.e.* gifts) between husband and wife are not subject to capital transfer tax whereas those between cohabitants are so subject.

The above brief account is concerned with the tax position of husband and wife whilst they are still living together. Once they separate or divorce the situation becomes more complex and financial orders are generally made with the taxation implications firmly in mind. These aspects cannot be dealt with in detail in the context of this book but they are noted *post* at p.92 in relation to financial orders on separation and divorce.

5. Social security

As with liability for tax, husbands and wives are also often treated as one unit for social security purposes. This approach is still paramount in relation to means-tested benefits, but it is slowly disappearing in relation to contributory benefits.

Certain benefits, notably unemployment, sickness and retirement benefits, are payable only if the claimant has paid the appropriate contributions. In the past a working married woman could choose to pay a special low rate of contribution. This meant that she was not entitled to any of the contributory benefits in her own right but she could qualify for a retirement or widow's pension on the basis of her husband's contribution record. The married woman's contribution rate was abolished for women entering employment from 1977 but there are still some women continuing under the old scheme. Now married women pay full contributions and qualify for all the contributory benefits in their own right. However, they still do not get the same benefits from the system as married men. First, a husband cannot rely on his wife's contributions in order to qualify for a retirement pension and does not qualify at all for a "widower's" pension. Secondly, a married woman who is receiving sickness or umemployment benefit will not receive any addition for a dependant child as long as she is living with her husband. She will only get the addition if separated or if her husband is "incapable of self support." Finally, she will not receive an addition for her husband unless he is, again, incapable of self support (Social Security Act 1975, ss. 44, 47 and 66). A married man is entitled to both a child and a spouse addition without having to prove any of these conditions.

The most important means-tested benefits are supplementary benefit (SB) and family income supplement (FIS). A wife who is residing with her husband will not generally be entitled to claim these means-tested benefits in her own right. The husband is the person entitled to claim. If he is entitled to benefit he will get extra money towards her support and for any children but his wife's resources will be added to his in determining entitlement. Therefore, in order to qualify for SB a husband will have to show that he satisfies all the conditions of entitlement and that his income and savings when added to those of his wife do not exceed the current rates of benefit. His wife will not be able to claim benefit at all. The same rule applies to unmarried couples who are living together as husband and wife (the "cohabitation" rule). Similar rules apply to FIS, which is a benefit designed to top up the pay of low paid full-time workers who are supporting children.

Once a husband and wife separate the wife is entitled to claim SB in her own right. However, if she does, the Department of Health and Social Security can take proceedings in the magistrates' court against the husband, as a "liable relative" for a contribution towards the maintenance of his wife (Supplementary Benefits Act 1976, s.18). The same rule applies to a wife—she is a "liable relative" who may be asked to contribute towards the maintenance of her separated husband if he is receiving benefit. In deciding how much a spouse should pay, the magistrates can make such order as they consider appropriate. The court will not normally order payments that would result in the payer's own means falling below subsistence level. An unresolved question concerns liability to maintain. Is it a good defence to an action brought by the DHSS for a husband to say that he is not liable to maintain his wife because of her conduct, such as desertion or adultery? It was suggested that this might be a defence in *NAB* v. *Parkes* (1955) but this old case predates the reforms in the general law relating to maintenance and there is some doubt if it is still good law.

For the effect of matrimonial financial orders on entitlement to SB see *post*, p.94.

6. Death

(a) *Wills*

Both spouses now enjoy the same capacity to make a will and enjoy complete testamentary freedom in the sense that neither is under any obligation to leave property to the other or to any other relative (but the terms of the will may be disregarded where there is a successful application under the Inheritance (Provision for Family and Dependants) Act 1975, see later).

A will made before marriage is revoked by marriage unless specifically made in contemplation of a particular marriage which takes place (Wills Act 1837, s.18; Law of Propery Act 1925, s.177). It must be possible to spell out of the contents and language of the will a reference to the particular marriage which ensued (*In the Estate of Langston* (1953)).

These rules are now embodied in the Administration of Justice Bill 1982, clause 18. The Bill also provides that where, after a will is made, the testator's marriage is dissolved or annulled, any bequest to the former spouse will lapse unless a contrary intention is shown in the will (see clause 18(2)). The Bill has not become law at the time of writing.

(b) *Intestacy*

A person who dies without making a valid will is said to die intestate. His assets pass to administrators who have a duty to distribute them (after meeting any liabilities) in accordance with the rules on intestacy (Administration of Estates Act 1925, as amended by the Intestates Estates Act 1952, Family Provision Act 1966 and Family Reform Act 1969). The rules are as follows:

(a) The rights of a surviving widow and widower are the same.
(b) The surviving spouse is entitled to the "personal chattels" (Act of 1925, s.55(1)(x)) of the deceased, provided the estate

is solvent and it is not necessary to sell them in order to pay debts and expenses.

(c) Any additional entitlement of a surviving spouse depends on whether the deceased has left issue or other relatives. If there are no surviving issue, parent, brother or sister of the whole blood or issue of theirs the surviving widow or widower is entitled to the whole of the residue. If there are children or remoter issue the survivor is entitled to a sum of up to £40,000 with interest at the rate of 4 per cent. from the date of death until payment, together with a life interest in half of the residue. If there are no children or other issue but a parent, brother, sister or issue of theirs the survivor is absolutely entitled to a sum of up to £85,000 with the same rate of interest and an absolute interest in half of the residue.

(d) The survivor has in certain circumstances rights of appropriation of the dwelling-house which was used as the matrimonial home when the deceased died (Act of 1952, Sched. 2).

(e) If the deceased is survived by a widow or widower and issue, the latter are entitled in equal shares to half of the residue and, subject to the survivor's life interest, to the other half on reaching the age of 18 or on marriage at an earlier age.

(f) The rights of a legitimate, an adopted and an illegitimate child are the same (subject to the latter's continuing inability to succeed to an entail or to take as "heir"). A legitimated child is entitled to an interest only in respect of an intestacy occurring after the date of his legitimation (Legitimacy Act 1976, s.5).

(c) *Family provision*

Freedom of testation can cause injustice to surviving members of the deceased's family, as can the rules which operate on intestacy. It was not until 1938 (Inheritance (Family Provision) Act) that the legislature sought to remedy this in relation to testate succession and only in 1952 (Intestates' Estates Act) were the provisions of the 1938 Act extended to intestacies.

The law is now governed by the Inheritance (Provision for Family and Dependants) Act 1975. An application for financial provision from the estate of a deceased person may be made within six months of the date when representation was taken out by the following persons:

(1) a spouse;
(2) a former spouse *who has not remarried*;

(3) a child of the deceased. This includes illegitimate children. Under the old law only infant or incapacitated sons and unmarried or incapacitated daughters could apply;

(4) a person who had been treated as a child of the family by the deceased (see p.95 for definition of child of the family. Note that the Act is *not* confined to infant children);

(5) "any person . . . who immediately before the death of the deceased was being maintained, either wholly or partly, by the deceased other than for full valuable consideration" (s.1(1)(*e*) and 1(3)). This would allow an application by, for example, a cohabitant or a relative, such as mother or sister, whom the deceased was supporting, providing they were not making equal contributions towards living expenses and the work of the household (see below).

In the case of an application by a surviving spouse the court can make such provision as is reasonable in all the circumstances and is not concerned simply with making provision for that spouse's maintenance alone. The spouse may have sufficient resources for his or her maintenance but it may well be unreasonable for the deceased spouse not to have made provision for him or her. In the case of all other applicants the court is concerned only with their reasonable maintenance (s. 1(2)). Thus, for example, a son well able to maintain himself to a reasonable standard would not be given further provision from his father's estate, even if such provision could normally have been expected by such a son under his father's will.

In all cases the court must examine all the circumstances including the net estate, the financial resources and needs of both the applicants and of the beneficiaries under the will or intestacy, and any physical or mental disability of the applicant or beneficiary. In the case of a child of the deceased the court must also consider what education or training he might have expected to receive, and in the case of a child of the family not a child of the deceased, the extent to which the deceased had assumed responsibility for his maintenance and whether or not the deceased knew the child was not his own (for similar provisions on divorce, see p.96).

Where an application is made by a *spouse* the Act specifically requires that the court make similar provision to that they would have made had the marriage ended in divorce rather than death (s.3(2); for financial provision on divorce see p.88). Thus the court will, presumably, use the "one-third rule" as a starting point, though this starting point may be thought inappropriate on death. However, the Act provides ample scope for modifying this approach.

In all cases the court should consider "any other matter" it considers relevant including the conduct of the applicant. It remains to be seen whether the courts will only concern themselves with "gross" bad conduct, as on divorce. It will often be difficult to calculate on death the provision that *would* have been made on divorce, and it may also be rather unhelpful to do so, because on divorce both spouses are living, continuing to receive income and capable of contracting further responsibilities such as a new spouse or children. Such considerations do not arise on the death of one partner.

The court has wider powers under the 1975 Act than under the previous law. Previously only periodical payments or lump sums could be ordered. Now, in addition, the court can order the transfer of specific property (*e.g.* the home) and also make settlements of any property in the estate. Also the court has wide powers to make provision for giving effect to their orders, for example it can order a sale of property, confer powers on trustees, etc. An order of periodic payments in favour of a former spouse or judicially separated spouse ceases on remarriage (s. 19(2)) but not an order in favour of a widow or widower. All orders for periodic payments may be varied. The court also has power to make interim orders to meet financial needs arising immediately after death but before a final order can be made (s. 5).

Applications for provision by dependants under s.1(1)(e) (see (5) above) of the Act have given rise to a number of problems. First, what does the applicant have to prove to show that he was being "maintained" by the deceased immediately before death? It has been held that the general relationship of the parties must be looked at, so that a person who had lived with the deceased for years would not be prevented from applying simply because the deceased had gone into hospital a few days or weeks before death and was not therefore maintaining the applicant in those weeks (*Re Beaumont* (1980)). Views have differed on whether it is necessary to show that the deceased did some act to show that he had assumed responsibility for the maintenance of the applicant. It was decided that this was necessary in *Re Beaumont* (1980). However, in *Jelley* v. *Iliffe* (1981) it was said that it was sufficient to show simply that maintenance was in fact provided. Finally, the maintenance must have been provided "other than for full valuable consideration." This phrase has caused considerable difficulty. It was intended to exclude housekeepers and paid companions from making a claim against the estate of their deceased employer. It can have the effect, however, of preventing an application by a deserving relative or cohabitee who, in return for free accommodation and some maintenance, renders housekeeping, nursing and other valuable services. It also prevents an application by a surviving cohabitee where the couple had pooled their more or less equal resources during their life together. The remaining cohabitee may not be able to prove that he or she was being maintained in these circumstances and, even if this hurdle is overcome, it will probably be alleged that the maintenance was provided for full valuable consideration. Because the result of a strict interpretation of sections 1(1)(e) and (3) would often be to exclude an application from the most deserving cases, some courts have been reasonably willing to find that the maintenance received by the applicant from the deceased exceeded in value any consideration provided for that maintenance (*Re Wilkinson* (1978)). However, in *Jelley* v. *Iliffe* (1981) the applicant had lived with the deceased in her house for eight years before her death. They pooled their retirement pensions to meet expenses and she cooked and washed for him. He provided some furniture and did odd jobs. It was held on appeal that the deceased, by providing valuable free accommodation, had assumed responsibility for his maintenance. The court sent the case back for trial because it was not clear whether the value of the consideration equalled or exceeded the value of the benefits provided by the deceased, but on balance it seemed likely that their contributions were equal.

(d) *Fatal accidents*

If the death of a husband or wife was caused by somebody's "wrongful act, neglect or default," certain surviving dependants may be able to claim compensation from the wrongdoer for their financial loss resulting from the deceased's death. Generally speaking it is the death of a breadwinner caused by somebody's negligence or an employer's actionable wrong which give rise to such claims, which were first introduced in the Fatal Accidents Act 1846 and are now governed by the Act of 1976.

Dependants on whose behalf a claim can be made are a husband or wife, child, stepchild or grandchild, whether legitmate, adopted, legitimated or illegitimate, father, mother, step-parent or grand-parent and the issue of any brother, sister, uncle or aunt of the deceased (1976 Act, s.1). The Administration of Justice Bill 1982, clause 3 adds a former wife or husband and certain cohabitants to this list. A claim can be made by a dependant only if the deceased himself, had he been injured instead of mortally wounded, could have maintained an action against the wrongdoer at the date of his death. By a similar principle any negligence by the deceased which contributed to his fatal accident reduces any damages recovered by a dependant in proportion to the degree of blame attaching to the deceased (1976 Act, s.5).

At the moment a claim under the Fatal Accidents Act does not lie for compensation for the bereavement, shock or suffering occasioned by the deceased's death but this will be made available once the Administration of Justice Bill 1982, clause 3 becomes law. Such a claim will be available to a husband, wife or child of the deceased and damages of £3,500 will be payable. The Act provides a remedy merely for reimbursement of funeral expenses and compensation for financial loss. This may be actual loss, like housekeeping money which ceased on death, or prospective loss of financial benefit which a dependant could reasonably expect to receive from the deceased if he had not been killed. Thus a wife who is separated from her husband and is not entitled to maintenance will recover under the Fatal Accidents Act only if she can prove that there was a real possibility that, but for the accident, the spouses would have become reconciled (*Davies* v. *Taylor* (1974)). A divorced spouse, even if in receipt of maintenance, cannot bring an action under the Act (*Payne-Collins* v. *Taylor Woodrow* (1975)) but will be able to do so once the Administration of Justice Bill 1982 becomes law. A cohabitant cannot recover under the Act, but the amount recovered by any children of the deceased that she looks after may be increased if they suffer loss as a consequence of the fact that their mother is not being maintained any more (*K.* v. *J. M. P.* (1975)). A wife's domestic services are for this purpose considered of pecuniary value to a surviving husband so that he is entitled to compensation for their loss (*Berry* v. *Humm & Co* (1915)). Since damages recoverable pursuant to a fatal accident claim are intended to compensate a dependant on a balance of gains and losses, any pecuniary benefit or reasonable expectation of benefit from the death of the deceased must be taken into account in reduction of any damages which would otherwise be awarded. Insurance money, benefits under the Social Security Act, any pension or gratuity which has been, will or may be paid as a result of the death are, however, excepted from this balance which the court has to strike (1976 Act, s.4).

The basic method of assessing damages recoverable in a claim under the Fatal Accidents Act is described in the following quotation from Lord Diplock's judgment in *Malyon* v. *Plummer* (1964):

> "Because in most cases the most reliable guide as to what would happen in the future if the deceased had lived is what did in fact happen in the past when he was alive, the common and convenient way of making the first estimate where the deceased at the time of his death was the breadwinner of the family is (a)

to ascertain what annual benefit in money or money's worth in fact accrued to the person for whom the action is brought from the deceased and arising out of the relationship before the death of the deceased; (b) to assess the extent (if any) to which that benefit would be likely to have increased or diminished in value in the future if the deceased had lived; (c)to assess the number of years for which that benefit would have been likely to have continued if the deceased had not been killed by the tortious act of the defendant; and (d) to apply to the annual benefit, assessed under (a) and (c) and generally called 'the dependancy', the appropriate multiplier derived from (c) allowance being made for the present receipt of a capital sum in respect of annual losses which would be sustained in the future. But the fact that it is convenient to have recourse to the past for guidance as to what would have been likely to happen in a hypothetical future which owing to the death of the deceased will never occur, must not blind one to the fact that one is estimating a loss which will be sustained in the future . . . The second estimate is in general . . . limited to pecuniary benefits to the person for whom the action is brought derived from the estate of the deceased . . . "

7. Contract, tort and crime

(a) *Contract*

Since the enactment of the Law Reform (Married Women and Tortfeasors) Act 1935 a married woman has the same contractual capacity as an unmarried woman. She and her husband can therefore not only independently enter into a contract with a stranger, but they are able to make a legally binding contract between themselves. An agreement between husband and wife is, however, a contract in the legal sense only if the evidence shows that in making it they intended their agreement to have legal force and consequences. Many "agreements" between a married couple are "domestic arrangements" of no legal significance.

The leading case on the distinction between a contract and a domestic arrangement is *Balfour's* case (1919). It arose from the promise made by a husband to pay his wife an allowance of £30 a month. He was an employee of the government of Ceylon and made this promise to his wife shortly before returning to Ceylon after spending his leave in England with her. She stayed behind on medical advice and when they parted they were on good terms and neither contemplated a permanent separation. Absence, however, took its toll and they never lived together again. At first the husband kept his promise regarding the monthly payments but in due course he defaulted with the result that his wife sued him for arrears owing.

The husband's defence to her claim was that his promise was in the circumstances not intended to be a legally enforceable contract.

(b) *Tort*

Since 1935 a husband and wife are each personally responsible and liable to pay compensation for committing a tort, and each in his own right can claim damages for being the victim of tort. (A tort is a civil wrong, the remedy for which is usually an award of damages.)

An action for damages for a tort committed by one party to a marriage against the other is, since the enactment of the Law Reform (Husband and Wife) Act 1962, allowed as if the parties were not married. Thus if a wife is injured by the negligent driving of her husband, she will be able to sue him in tort for damages, and thus take advantage of the husband's insurance cover. The court may stay such proceedings during the subsistence of a marriage if satisfied that no substantial benefit would accrue to either party from the continuation of the proceedings. This power of the court is intended to prevent a married couple suing each other out of spite and for petty and trifling complaints within the scope of ordinary wear and tear of married life. The Act also provides a procedural power to stay proceedings in order to ensure the most convenient disposal of any issue between married parties.

(c) *Crime*

Criminal law applies to married and unmarried persons and to husbands and wives alike, but a wife is entitled to the benefit of a special statutory defence to all charges other than treason and murder. It entitles her to an acquittal if she proves that the offence for which she stands charged was committed in the presence of and under the coercion of her husband (Criminal Justice Act 1925, s.47).

Since the enactment of the Theft Act 1968 a husband and wife are now able to prosecute each other for any offence whatever as if they were not married (s. 30 (2)), subject to the consent of the Director of Public Prosecutions for the prosecution of either for stealing from the other or for doing unlawful damage to the other's property, unless the accused's spouse is charged with committing the offence jointly with a stranger or the spouses were at the time of the alleged offence no longer under a duty to cohabit by virtue of a decree of judicial separation or other order to the same effect (s. 30(4)).

In criminal proceedings instituted by one party against the other the prosecuting spouse may give evidence for the prosecution (s. 30(2)). He or she may do so also as a witness for the prosecution or the defence if the other spouse is prosecuted (other than by the witness himself) for committing any offence with reference to the witness or the witness' property. If the offence is one of personal violence the witness is compellable and must answer all relevant questions. In all other cases the witness cannot be compelled to give evidence, but if he or she volunteers to do so the witness is not bound to disclose any communication made to her or him during the marriage by the accused and the witness' failure to give evidence may not be made the subject of any comment by the prosecution (s.30(3)).

In civil proceedings there is no longer any privilege relating to communication between spouses during marriage (Civil Evidence Act 1968, s.16(3)).

Part II

BREAKDOWN OF MARRIAGE

Introduction

When a marriage breaks down the intervention of the courts is generally required to regulate the status of the spouses, their rights and claims to property and their relationship with their children. The law in England does little to encourage reconciliation though in recent years reforms in the law on divorce and maintenance have been framed with the purpose of reducing friction and bitterness between separated spouses.

On breakdown of marriage the parties may have immediate problems with the home, money or children that cannot wait for a solution until a divorce is heard. The available remedies are dealt with in Chapter 3. For most couples the breakdown of a marriage will lead to divorce (Chapter 6), but petitioning for nullity (Chapter 7) may be another option. Equally those who do not, for religious or other reasons, wish to terminate their marriage may either make their own separation agreement (Chapter 4) or petition for a judicial separation (Chapter 6). Whatever solution is chosen it will be necessary to sort out the spouses' future financial position. This is dealt with in Chapter 8. Children are the subject of Part III of this book.

Chapter 3

IMMEDIATE PROBLEMS AND EMERGENCY REMEDIES

Long before either spouse has obtained a divorce, or even decided to petition for one, problems may arise relating to the occupation of the home, personal protection and maintenance. Similarly it may be urgently necessary to seek the assistance of the court on the custody of or access to children. This chapter is concerned with the orders that can be made prior to a final decree of divorce or judicial separation, or where no other matrimonial relief is being sought. In particular it is concerned with the orders that can be made quickly, in an emergency.

1. The Home

There are numerous ways in which the right to occupy the home can be regulated. These are:

(i) an application to the court under the Matrimonial Homes Act 1967, s.1, see *ante* p.25.

(ii) an application to the county court for an injunction against molestation or excluding the other spouse from the home or permitting the applicant spouse to enter it.

(iii) an application to the magistrates' court for a personal protection order or an exclusion order.

(iv) an application to the High Court for an injunction, similar to those available in the county court.

In many of these cases there will be an element of urgency, often extreme urgency, where a wife or child have been violently treated, and in all cases except under heading (i) above there is some provision for obtaining an order quickly. All these remedies overlap and which one is chosen depends on speed, convenience and the availability of legal aid. Most cases are dealt with in the county court or magistrates' courts under headings (ii) and (iii) above and these will be dealt with in this chapter.

(a) *Injunctions in the county court*

County courts have always had a general power to issue injunctions against molestation or to evict a spouse from the home where this was necessary to protect a spouse or a child. In general these injunctions would be granted only where there were pending matrimonial proceedings, such as where a petition for divorce had been issued. The order would last until the matrimonial litigation had been finally dealt with when, of course, the court would have the power to make a final order dealing with the home (*Bassett* (1975)). This jurisdiction still exists but there are a number of problems associated with it. First, matrimonial proceedings had to be started before an injunction could be applied for. This meant that a "battered wife" in need of immediate protection was required to launch divorce or other proceedings as a preliminary to asking for protection or sole occupation of the home. Secondly, the court cannot protect cohabitants under this jurisdiction as, of course, they are unable to launch matrimonial proceedings.

The Domestic Violence and Matrimonial Proceedings Act 1976 was passed to deal with these problems and also with problems related to enforcement of orders. It provides that the court may grant an injunction to either party "whether or not any other relief is sought in the proceedings."

What has to be proved. The Act lays down no statutory conditions for obtaining an injunction so the order is entirely within the court's discretion. A series of cases in the House of Lords and the Court of Appeal in the last five years have given some guidance although obviously each case depends very much on its own facts.

First, it is not necessary to prove violence although proof of violence will make the granting of an order more likely. The courts will consider primarily the welfare of any children and their need to live securely and without stress with the custodial parent in the home. In *Davis* v. *Johnson* (1978) Lord Scarman said "the mischief against which Parliament has legislated . . . may be described in these terms: conduct by a family partner which puts at risk the security, or sense of security, of the other partner in the home. Physical violence, or the threat of it, is clearly within the mischief. But there is more than that to it. Homelessness can be as great a threat to the security of a woman (or man) and her children."

In *Walker* (1978) there was no violence but serious friction between husband and wife which affected the children. Life together had become impossible and, as it was clear that the wife had to look after the children, the court ordered the husband to leave the home. (See also *Spindlow* (1979) and *Rennick* (1977).) However the court will be loath to make an order if it considers that the applicant merely finds it inconvenient to live with the other spouse or if it thinks that the application for an injunction is simply a tactical manoeuvre connected with divorce proceedings (*Bassett* (1975); *Masich* (1977)). Some evidence of adverse or bad conduct on the part of the spouse to be excluded may be required, though there are conflicting Court of Appeal decisions on this point (compare *Elsworth* (1979) with *Harding* (1980)).

Application to cohabitants. Cohabitants are covered by the Act but some particular problems have arisen in relation to them. The Act states that it applies to "a man and a woman who are living with each other in the same household as husband and wife" (s.1(2)). What is the position if the woman leaves the home because of the man's violence and then applies for an injunction to exclude him and allow her to return? She is not, at the time of her application, living with him as his wife. Nevertheless it has been held that the Act applies in such circumstances (*Davis* v. *Johnson* (1978)) though it is not known how quickly such a woman should act before losing her right to apply. In *McLean* v. *Nugent* (1979) the parties had been apart for three months but the woman was still able to get an injunction ousting the man. It was also held in *Davis* v. *Johnson* that a cohabitant can obtain an injunction to evict the other partner even though the applicant has no proprietorial or other interest in the home. (A spouse has rights of occupation under the Matrimonial Homes Act 1967 which do not extend to cohabitants.) Finally it was held in *Adeoso* (1980) that a cohabitant could apply for an order under the Act even where the couple were living entirely separate lives although under the same roof. The parties in this case had been living together but had become estranged.

Injunctions and property rights. It has been frequently stated that the grant of an injunction evicting a person from the home does not affect property rights. The tenant or owner of the home will continue to be such whether or not an order is in force preventing him from occupying it (*Davis* v. *Johnson*). He will therefore continue to be liable for mortgage or rent payments. An injunction will not generally last for more than three months or until any pending proceedings relating to the home have been dealt with. On divorce or judicial separation it is of course possible for the home to be transferred from one spouse to the other. No such possibility exists in relation to unmarried couples so, after the injunction comes to an end, the evicted partner is free to return if he has a legal or equitable interest in the home. Where a spouse or partner becomes homeless as a consequence of actual or threatened domestic violence, the local authority will have a duty to rehouse, either temporarily or permanently, provided the homeless partner has responsibility for caring for the children (Housing (Homeless Persons) Act 1977, s.1).

Enforcement. Breach of an order constitutes contempt of court for which the court can, on a subsequent application by the applicant, impose a term of imprisonment. However a more effective method of enforcement is for the police to arrest the defendant immediately a breach occurs or is threatened. This can be done if the court attaches a power of arrest to the order when it is made (1976 Act, s.2(1)). This may be attached if the defendant has actually caused physical harm to the applicant or a child and where he is likely to do so again. It is not a routine remedy and will be granted only where it is shown to be needed for the protection of the applicant or a child (*Lewis* (1978)). A police officer is then empowered to arrest a person suspected of being in breach, or threatening to commit a breach, of the order. The arrested person must be brought before the court within 24 hours of arrest.

Ex parte orders. County courts can act very quickly in making these orders. An *ex parte* order is one which is made without the other side being told of the hearing or being given an opportunity to be present. Such orders will last for only a few days until a proper hearing can be arranged. Courts are very unwilling to order *ex parte exclusions* orders, although a power to do so exists. *Ex parte* orders are therefore generally confined to non-molestation injunctions.

(b) *Magistrates' court orders*

Magistrates have had the power to make personal protection orders and exclusion orders since November 1979 when sections 16–18 of the Domestic Proceedings and Magistrates' Courts Act 1978 came into force. These sections replace the largely ineffective non-cohabitation order that magistrates were able to make under the old law.

A *protection order* may be made if it is proved that: (i) the respondent has used or threatened to use violence against a spouse or child of the family, and (ii) that it is necessary to make the order in order to protect that spouse or child.

An *exclusion order* whereby a respondent can be ordered to leave the home, refrain from entering it or allow the applicant to enter it, can be made if one of the following more stringent conditions are satisfied:

   (i) the respondent has committed violence to spouse or child, or
  (ii) the respondent has threatened violence to spouse or child and committed it against someone else, or
 (iii) the respondent has threatened violence against spouse or child in breach of an existing protection order.

In addition to one of these conditions it must be proved that the spouse or child is in danger of physical injury (though it is not necessary to prove that the danger is immediate (*McCartney* (1981))).

The stress in all these conditions is on violence, or the threat of it, and physical injury. It can be seen therefore that the powers of the magistrates' courts are much more circumscribed than are those of the county court. In particular the magistrates would not be able to make an order in cases like *Walker* or *Spindlow* noted on p.46.

Magistrates also have the power to act quickly. Expedited protection orders may be made by a single justice where there is an immediate danger of physical injury. The order can be made even though the summons has not been served on the respondent, or where the date fixed for the hearing in the summons has not yet arrived. Expedited orders will last for up to 28 days. It is *not* possible to obtain an expedited *exclusion* order however—which is often the very order that the applicant wants to obtain with maximum speed.

A power of arrest can be attached to the order as in the county courts under the Domestic Violence and Matrimonial Proceedings Act 1976. Otherwise a breach of an order will be enforced in the usual way in magistrates' courts, namely committal for up to two months or a fine of up to £50 for each day of default up to a maximum of £1,000 (1978 Act, s.78(1)).

Obviously the jurisdiction of the county courts and the magistrates' courts overlap. Which one will be chosen by the applicant depends not only on the facts of the individual case—violence being essential in the magistrates' court—but also on the proximity of the local court, the speed with which it can or will act and the availability of legal aid. At the time of writing it is not known how popular the new magistrates' jurisdiction will prove to be.

2. Maintenance

A spouse, especially a wife whose marriage has broken up, may be in urgent need of money. There is, however, no quick "emergency" procedure for applying for maintenance. An application can be made to the magistrates' court as described in Chapter 5, or to the county court for maintenance pending suit (see p.87). However it may take some weeks before the court makes an order. A person who is destitute has therefore to turn to the DHSS and ask for supplementary benefit.

Another immediate problem that may arise concerns the preservation of the assets of the family. A wife may fear that her husband will transfer assets or dispose of property so as to prevent her making any claim to them on divorce. This can be prevented if immediate action is taken by bringing proceedings under section 37 of the Matrimonial Causes Act 1973 as described on p. 99).

3. Children

When a marriage breaks up the children may be in danger of violence or other harmful conduct from one of the spouses. In such cases the children can be protected if the other spouse applies for an order under the Domestic Violence Act or the Domestic Proceedings and Magistrates' Courts Act 1978 as already described. These provisions are designed to protect children just as much as spouses.

Where one spouse fears that a child may be "kidnapped" by the other or taken out of the country the only effective remedy is to make the child a ward of court. The court can then order that the child be brought before it and also that it is not removed from the jurisdiction, as described in Chapter 12.

CHAPTER 4

SEPARATION AGREEMENTS

It is obviously better if a couple whose marriage is breaking down can come to an agreement between themselves rather than go to court. Separation and maintenance agreements are valid provided they satisfy the conditions outlined below. There may, however, be tax reasons for converting an agreement into a court consent order on divorce or judicial separation (see *Minton* (1979)).

A separation agreement between a husband and wife is valid provided the agreement takes effect either immediately it is made or it is made by spouses who have been apart and are attempting a reconciliation. Such couples may want to regulate a possible future separation if the reconciliation fails. An agreement to separate in the future in any other case is regarded as being against public policy and is void (*Re Meyrick's Settlement* (1921)).

Spouses can make an oral separation agreement but the agreement must be in writing if either of them wish to invoke the court's powers to vary it under the Matrimonial Causes Act 1973, s.35. Where an agreement contains financial arrangements it is wise to make it under seal for taxation reasons.

The actual terms of an agreement depend entirely on the requirements of the parties concerned and the language employed to express those terms is not standardised. The effect of no two agreements is therefore likely to be the same. The following are merely examples of the type of clauses commonly found in separation agreements.

1. Agreement to live separately

This is a standard term in agreements which releases the parties from the duty to cohabit. It should not be included if in fact both spouses are not agreed on the separation as such an agreement terminates desertion (see p.70).

2. Non molestation clause

The spouses agree not to molest, annoy or disturb the other, a clause which can be enforced by an injunction.

3. Maintenance

Agreements may contain clauses regulating the maintenance of both the spouses and the children. Where a spouse is concerned this clause often contains what is known as a "dum casta" clause, limiting the liability to pay maintenance for as long as a wife remains "chaste," *i.e.* does not commit adultery or live with another man.

An agreement not to apply to a court for maintenance for either a spouse or a child is void. Nobody can be prevented from applying to the court for financial relief (though of course the application may fail for want of merit) (Matrimonial Causes Act 1973, s.34(1); *Hyman* (1924); *Re M.* (1968)). This inability to promise not to upset the basis of what is intended to be a final agreement by going to court often causes difficulties. Many husbands, for example, would be willing to transfer ownership of the home to their wives if they can be sure that by so doing they have finally discharged their financial liabilities to them. The only way to achieve such finality is to get the court to make an order on divorce finally dismissing a wife's claims to periodical payments (see further p.91).

4. Custody and access to children

There is nothing to prevent husbands and wives making agreements on custody and access on separation (Guardianship Act 1973, s.1(2)). However these agreements will not be enforced if the court considers them to be contrary to the best interests of the child.

Variation of agreements

The parties to an agreement can at any time mutually agree to vary its terms without resort to lawyers or a court. In default of an agreed variation an agreement continues in force for its agreed duration unless, on an application by either party under sections 35–36 of the Matrimonial Causes Act 1973, a court orders an alteration in the agreement. The court's powers of variation apply only to an agreement in writing which is either a separation agreement without financial arrangements (where there is no other written agreement containing such arrangements) or an agreement containing financial arrangements whether made during the continuance or after the dissolution or annulment of the marriage, and they are exercisable only if a court is satisfied either—

"(a) that by reason of a change in the circumstances in the light of which any financial arrangements contained in the agreement were made or, as the case may be, financial arrangements were omitted from it (including a change foreseen by the parties when making the agreement), the agreement should be altered so as to contain financial arrangements, or

(b) that the agreement does not contain proper financial arrangements with respect to any child of the family."

A court's powers to make alterations in an agreement are restricted to either varying or revoking any financial arrangements agreed, or to inserting financial provisions for the benefit of one of the parties or of a child of the family where none had been agreed. A variation may be backdated (*Warden* (1981)). Financial provision ordered on variation must, in respect of an ex-wife, cease on her remarriage and in respect of a child must not exceed what a court can order in proceedings for divorce, nullity or judicial separation (see p.95). Subject to these restrictions a court may make such orders "as may appear . . . to be just having regard to all the circumstances."

Application for the variation of an agreement may be made to the High Court, a divorce county court or a magistrates' court. The jurisdiction of magistrates is limited to varying provisions involving periodical payments and they can entertain an application only if both parties are resident in England and at least one of them lives within the area of the court. The jurisdiction of the other courts may be exercised if each of the parties is either domiciled or resident in England and Wales.

Application for variation may be made after the death of one of the parties to an agreement if the deceased died domiciled in England and the financial arrangements under the agreement continue beyond death. Such an application must be made to the High Court and, except with the permission of the court, not later than six months after the date on which representation in regard to the estate of the deceased is first taken out.

Termination
Events or behaviour by either party after the making of an agreement may result in its discharge due to the operation of the general principles of the law of contract, which apply to separation and maintenance agreements as they do to any other legal contract. A breach of an agreement by either party does not therefore terminate it, unless the breach is so serious or fundamental as to show an intention by the party in breach of no longer being bound by the terms of the agreement and the other party exercises the option of treating it as discharged (*Pardy* (1939)). Matrimonial proceedings or a temporary resumption of cohabitation with a view to a reconciliation are other typical situations raising the question whether an agreement is still in force. The answer depends on the true construction of each agreement (*Adams* (1941)).

CHAPTER 5

MATRIMONIAL ORDERS IN THE MAGISTRATES' COURTS

The magistrates' courts were the forum which provided some help for those in the lowest income groups whose marriages were breaking down. Their powers were, however, limited. They could order payment of weekly maintenance and custody of or access to children up to the age of 16. They could *not* make orders relating to property or order lump sums and neither could they make any order relating to the occupation of the home. The "non cohabitation clause" which could be inserted into magistrates' courts orders was simply an order that the parties were no longer legally obliged to live together. It provided no protection at all for a wife in fear of violence or other molestation. The law which applied in the magistrates' courts became seriously outdated after 1971, when the Divorce Law Reform Act 1969 came into force. It was based on fault—applicants had to prove one of a possible nine matrimonial "offences." An adulterous wife was absolutely barred from obtaining relief and an offence which was "condoned" or "connived at" could not form the basis of a complaint. As the Finer Committee said in 1974:

> " . . . whereas the substantive law of divorce gives effect to modern and enlightened principles of public policy, the substantive matrimonial law administered by magistrates is still largely based on the public policy of the latter part of the nineteenth century."

The solution proposed in the Finer Report was the abolition of the domestic jurisdiction of magistrates' courts, and its replacement with a properly integrated Family Court system. This solution, however, was regarded as too costly. Instead, the law in the magistrates' courts was reformed by the Domestic Proceedings and Magistrates' Courts Act of 1978, the bulk of which came into force in February 1981. This Act was proposed in the Law Commission's Report No.77, 1976.

The magistrates' courts domestic jurisdiction has been steadily decreasing in popularity. In 1970 there were 27,905 matrimonial complaints, in 1979 it was 3,650. Much of the existing business of the courts consists of the enforcement of orders made by the county courts on divorce rather than the making of original orders. An important cause of the decline in the popularity of the magistrates' courts was a change in the policy of the Supplementary Benefits Commission (SBC) who were responsible for the administration of supplementary benefit. About half of the wives who applied to the magistrates' courts for maintenance were in receipt of SB and it is clear that many of them made the application because of pressure to do so from the SBC. The order rarely provided the wife with any financial advantage because the amount of her SB would be reduced by the amount of maintenance she received. In 1975 the SBC agreed not to pressurise wives into taking these proceedings and the legal aid authorities became most unwilling to finance proceedings that brought the legally aided wife no real benefit. As a result of this change in policy the number of proceedings in magistrates' courts dropped.

1. Powers of the magistrates' courts

The magistrates still do not have the power to terminate marriages. Nor do they have the power any more to make non-cohabitation orders. As this order was effectively unenforceable and was *not* the equivalent of a non-molestation order (see p.48), it was considered to be of doubtful utility and therefore abolished in the 1978 Act.

The orders that can be made under the 1978 Act are:

(1) maintenance: an order that the respondent to pay periodical maintenance and/or a lump sum of up to £500 to the complainant or the children (see further p.56);
(2) custody of and access to children (see further p.57);
(3) a personal protection order (see p.48);
(4) an order excluding the respondent from the matrimonial home (see p.48).

2. Grounds for an order

Either spouse may make an application for maintenance in the magistrates' courts on one or more of three basic grounds:

(a) failure to provide maintenance for the applicant or any child of the family;
(b) behaviour which the applicant cannot reasonably be expected to live with;
(c) desertion.

(section 1 of the 1978 Act).
In addition an order can be made:

(d) by consent under section 6;
(e) where the parties have been separated for three months and the respondent has been making maintenance payments to the applicant or children, under section 7.

The first ground, neglect to maintain, is new. Under the old law it was necessary to prove "wilful" neglect to maintain, which meant that no order would be made against a respondent who did not know that his spouse was in need, or who reasonably thought he was not liable to maintain her. The two other grounds, behaviour and desertion, bear the same meaning as in divorce (see p.67), except that it is not necessary to establish a period of desertion of two years. The fourth ground allows the magistrates for the first time to make consent orders. It is beneficial from both the point of view of enforcement and liability for tax that maintenance should be paid as a result of a court order rather than mutual agreement alone. A consent order allows this without requiring the parties to parade their matrimonial problems before the court. It appears that a lump sum provision contained in a consent order can exceed the normal magistrates' court limit of £500. The court will not agree to a consent order if it considers that the provision made for any children is inadequate. The final ground is a complex one and will probably be little used. It is designed to assist the wife who is separated from her husband (neither of them being in desertion) and who *is* maintained to get the security of a court order for maintenance.

None of the old defences to the making of an order—adultery, connivance and condonation—are re-enacted in the 1978 Act. The only defences therefore will be either proof that desertion or unreasonable behaviour are not established (see p.67) or that the applicant was being reasonably maintained by the respondent.

3. Orders that can be made

(a) *Financial*
Periodical payments or lump sums may be ordered in favour of both the applicant and any child of the family. The lump sum cannot exceed £500 but it appears that the magistrates are not limited to ordering one lump sum, as are the divorce courts. This power to order a lump sum, which is new, may be particularly useful to a wife whose husband has left her with rent, fuel or other bills to pay. However, she will have to take care that the receipt of such a lump sum does not simply reduce any supplementary benefit to which she might be entitled.

The principles upon which the amount of maintenance should be assessed for both spouses and children are contained in section 3 of the 1978 Act and are very similar to those in section 25 of the Matrimonial Causes Act 1973 (on which see p.88). Obviously, however, the magistrates are not concerned with the final termination of the marriage.

In their Report the Law Commission expressed the hope that the conduct of the parties should be taken into account only if it was "obvious and gross" as laid down in the case of *Wachtel* (1973). It is clear from section 3(2) of the Act that the conduct of the spouse is entirely irrelevant where maintenance for the *children* is being considered and it has been held that maintenance should not be reduced because a custodial spouse is being difficult about access (*R. v. Halifax Justices, ex p. Woolveston* (1978)). A maintenance order can be made payable directly to a child (1978 Act, section 2(1)) which can have tax advantages (see p.93).

Another innovation contained in the 1978 Act is that maintenance orders can now be applied for whilst the spouses are still living together. Such an order will, however, cease to be enforceable if the parties continue to cohabit for more than six months. Equally, if an order is made whilst the parties are living apart, it will remain in force for six months if they live together again.

Maintenance for children can be ordered even if the complainant fails to establish one of the grounds set out in section 1 of the 1978 Act. The order can be made against either the complainant or the respondent. If custody is given to a third party, such as a grandparent or other relative, no maintenance order in relation to the children can be made. An order can, however, be made in relation to a child committed to the care of a local authority (1978 Act, s.11).

(b) *Custody and access*

Wherever a spouse applies for a financial order the court *must* consider whether or not to make an order in relation to any child of the family (for the definition see p.95) (s.8(1)). The parties themselves may not have applied for custody or access, but the court still has a duty to consider these matters. A custody order may be made in respect of any child up to 18 years old. Custody may be given to a third party (*e.g.* a grandmother or other relative). Joint custody orders are not theoretically available under the 1978 Act (s.8(4)) but the same effect of a joint order can be achieved by giving custody to one parent but ordering that the other shall "retain all or such as the court may specify of the parental rights and duties comprised in legal custody (other than the right to the actual custody of the child)." These "reserved" parental rights must be exercised jointly with the parent given legal custody (s.8(4)). Any dispute between the parents on the exercise of these rights must be resolved by the court (1978 Act, s.13). The court can also make a supervision order in relation to the children (s.9), and may also commit the child to the care of the local authority in "exceptional circumstances" (1978 Act, s.10). Either spouse may be awarded access and so may a parent of the child. For example if the child is the child of one of the parties to the marriage, the court could make an access order in favour of the child's other natural parent (1978 Act, s.8(2)). No other person may be awarded access except where an application is made by a grandparent under section 14. This provides that where the court is considering making an order in relation to children under section 8, or where such an order is in force, a grandparent may apply for access and the court can make such order for access as it thinks fit. It should be noted that a grandparent cannot initiate such an application unless the spouses have already gone to the magistrates' court for an order. It is essentially a right to intervene in existing proceedings; a similar right exists in relation to divorce proceedings.

4. Variation or termination of orders

Orders for periodical payments may be revoked or varied under section 20 of the 1978 Act. A periodical payment order can be varied by making instead an order for the payment of a lump sum (s.20(1)). Orders for lump sum payments cannot be varied or revoked but there appears to be no reason why a new application for another lump sum should not be made (the county courts on divorce can only order one lump sum).

Orders cannot last for longer than the joint lives of the parties, but will remain enforceable after divorce or nullity unless an application to vary or revoke is made. Orders cease to be enforceable after the remarriage of the party receiving maintenance (s.4).

5. Enforcement

The enforcement processes for an order requiring the payment of money are now to be found in the Magistrates' Courts Act 1980. The great advantage of the magistrates' courts is that the clerk can undertake the business of enforcement if the written consent of the unpaid complainant is obtained (1980 Act, s.32(1)). There is no comparable machinery for delegating enforcement in any other court. However, both the High and county courts provide additional methods of enforcement (by proceeding directly against bank accounts or property for example) which are not available in the magistrates' courts.

It should be noted that maintenance arrears are not automatically enforceable like any other civil debt. The court can remit the whole or part of any sum due (1980 Act, s.95). In general the court should not enforce the payment of arrears which have accrued more than a year before the enforcement application (*Ross* v. *Pearson* (1976)).

Maintenance can be enforced by a distress order on the respondent's goods (which is little used), by an attachment of earnings order or by committal to prison.

Attachment of earnings

This method of enforcing payments under a maintenance order was introduced by the Maintenance Orders Act 1958 and is now governed by the Attachment of Earnings Act 1971. The defendant himself may apply for an attachment order (1971 Act, s.3(1)) but where the complainant applies, which is the more usual situation, the following conditions must be satisfied. An order is not available as a means of enforcement until at least 15 days have elapsed since the maintenance order was made and the defendant has failed to pay one or more instalments. The defendant must be present in court and the magistrates must be satisfied that his failure to pay is due to "wilful refusal" or "culpable neglect" (s.3(5)).

The result of an order is a direction from the court to the defendant's employer to pay to the court the sum, known as the "normal deduction rate," that the court thinks is reasonable to deduct to meet the maintenance liability. The order must also specify the "protected earnings rate," which is the sum below which the debtor's earnings must not be allowed to fall (Act of 1971, s.6(5)).Failure by an employer to comply with the court's direction is an offence punishable by a fine.

The making of an attachment of earnings order, therefore, involves the determination by the court of two amounts: first, the protected earnings rate which is the amount below which 'having regard to the resources and needs of the defendant and the needs of persons for whom he must or reasonably may provide," the defendant's earnings due to him must in no circumstances be reduced; and, secondly, the normal deduction rate, which is the amount considered reasonable by the court to satisfy payments as they fall due under the related maintenance order plus payment of the arrears by instalments within a reasonable period. If a defendant's earnings on any pay day are less than the amount of the protected earnings rate, the deficiency must be made up by the employer out of future earnings in preference to payment to the court of the normal deduction rate and of any arrears which have accrued under it. Subject to this, any surplus is payable to the court in reduction of underpayments of the deduction rate. In fixing the protected earnings rate the debtor's take home pay should not fall below subsistence level and, as a guide, the court can consider the current rates for supplementary benefit. However, the court can, if it is reasonable, fix a protected earnings rate at a sum lower than the level of supplementary benefit (*Billington* (1974)).

An attachment of earnings order lapses on notice from an employer to the court that a defendant whose wages are subject to the attachment has left his employment but may be redirected to a new employer (s.9(4)). The debtor is under a duty to inform the court of any change of employment, and a new employer is under a duty to inform the court if he knows that an attachment order exists against any new employee (s.15).

Committal to prison

A defendant may be sent to prison only if a court, after inquiry in his presence, decides that his default is due to either his wilful refusal or his culpable neglect to pay what is owing under the court order (Maintenance Orders Act 1958, s.16, and Administration of Justice Act 1970, s.12)). The minimum period of imprisonment is five days; the maximum six weeks. It is unusual for a defendant to be sent to prison without first being given a further opportunity of paying the current weekly amount and the arrears by specified instalments. This is done by means of a "suspended committal order" imposing a contingent period of imprisonment which need not be served as long as a defendant complies with the condition of suspension.

Serving a sentence of imprisonment does not extinguish any arrears owing. On the other hand a defendant cannot be sent to prison more than once for failure to pay the same sum of money and, unless a court orders otherwise, no further arrears accrue while he is in prison. On application by a defaulting defendant the court has wide powers to review and to vary committal orders and, if it thinks fit, to remit any arrears wholly or in part (Magistrates' Court Act 1980, s.95). Committal to prison and an order for the attachment of earnings are mutually exclusive modes of enforcement and cannot co-exist. If a court is in a position to order either it must not impose imprisonment unless it considers an attachment order inappropriate.

Enforcing non financial orders

Orders other than those for the payment of money are enforced by levying fines upon the defaulter. The fines may be up to £50 for every day in default, but not exceeding £1,000 in total. Alternatively the defaulter may be committed to prison for up to two months (Domestic Proceedings and Magistrates' Courts Act 1978, s.78).

6. Registration and variation of divorce court orders

This forms a very significant part of the present workload of the magistrates' courts in domestic matters. Divorce court maintenance orders may be registered and thereafter enforced through the magistrates' courts. About 20,000 such orders are registered. There are two main reasons for registration. The first is to take advantage of the easier method of enforcement used in the court, in particular the active role of the clerk in the process (see *ante*, p.58). The second is that registered orders may be "diverted" to the DHSS if the recipient is on supplementary benefit. This means that the court pays over directly to the DHSS whatever maintenance is received from the husband. The DHSS will pay the wife her full entitlement to benefit, whatever maintenance is or is not received from the husband. The wife is then not at the mercy of irregularly paid maintenance but receives a consistent amount of benefit each week. The diversion procedure can be used only if the maintenance order is for the same amount as, or less than, the benefit to which the wife is entitled. Over 40 per cent. of wives with maintenance orders are receiving supplementary benefit and orders are very irregularly complied with. Of those made or registered in the magistrates' courts in 1970 only 45 per cent. were regularly complied with, 15 per cent. were irregularly complied with and 40 per cent. were almost never paid at all(Finer Report (1974), p.98).

7. Procedure

Applications are made to the specially constituted domestic bench of the magistrates' court where either of the parties normally reside. The court must be kept separate from the criminal business of the magistrates' courts. The bench must have at least one man and one woman. Complaints are made on a simple form which requires brief details of the circumstances supporting the complaint (Matrimonial Proceedings Rules 1980, S.I. 1980 No. 1582). The defendant is then served with a summons which gives notice of the nature of the complaint and the date and time fixed for the hearing. The procedure after this follows the normal pattern for all judicial proceedings. The court, however, sits in private although members of the press are permitted to attend. Press reports must not give particulars of the case other than a concise statement of the parties' names, the charges, the result and the observations of the court in giving their decision. Publication of evidence is forbidden (Magistrates' Courts Act 1980, s.82).

The domestic courts are the only courts where representation by a solicitor can be paid for by the legal aid fund under the more informal "advice and assistance" scheme (also known as the "green form scheme") rather than the civil legal aid scheme normally used for litigation. The advice and assistance scheme involves a simpler means test which is administered by the solicitor himself rather than the legal aid authorities.

Appeals from the decisions of the magistrates' court go to the Family Division of the High Court.

Chapter 6

DIVORCE AND JUDICIAL SEPARATION

A divorce terminates a marriage leaving the parties free to contract another marriage; judicial separation is simply an order of the court that the spouses live apart. Comparatively few judicial separations are applied for nowadays (in 1980 it was 5,423) but they are useful for those who have religious objections to divorce. On making an order for judicial separation the court is able to make exactly the same orders on property, maintenance, custody and access as on divorce.

Over 177,415 petitions for divorce were presented in 1980 and virtually all of them were successful. The defended divorce action is almost a thing of the past – just over 1,000 cases were set down as defended in 1979. One reason for this is undoubtedly that most spouses recognise the futility of defending a petition when ultimately a divorce will be almost inevitable on separation grounds. Secondly, it is no longer necessary, as it used to be, to raise issues of conduct in divorce proceedings in order to preserve the right to raise those issues in proceedings for financial relief. Conduct is, in any case, far less relevant to all proceedings, including those for financial relief, than it used to be. Procedure for divorce is now so simple, most cases being dealt with by the "special procedure" which involves no court hearing, that it seems to be almost an administrative formality. It is not surprising therefore that few cases now reach the courts on the substantive law on divorce and that it has developed little since the early 1970s when the Divorce Law Reform Act of 1969 came into force. It is nevertheless necessary to know the law on the grounds for divorce as one cannot be obtained, even by an administrative procedure, unless the petitioner can establish in the approved manner that he or she has a legal basis for a decree.

A. Divorce

1. Restrictions on petitions within three years of marriage

A petition for divorce may not be presented before the expiration of three years from the date of the marriage unless a judge has given leave for proceedings to be started within that period "on the ground that the case is one of exceptional hardship suffered by the petitioner or of exceptional depravity on the part of the respondent" (Matrimonial Causes Act 1973, s.3). It is not necessary to prove *both* exceptional hardship and exceptional depravity. This provision is designed to prevent haste in getting divorced, and to encourage reconciliation while there is hope. The Act directs the judge when dealing with an application to "have regard to the interest of any . . . child and to the question whether there is reasonable probability of a reconciliation between the parties . . . " In *Re S.* (1978), Simon P. considered that in appropriate cases the court should adjourn an application for the purpose of attempting a reconciliation with the help of the court welfare officers. (See also section 6(2) of the Matrimonial Causes Act.)

In recent years the courts have taken an increasingly relaxed attitude to the need to prove exceptional hardship or depravity, although each case obviously depends very much on its own acts. In *Bowman* (1949) Lord Denning gave examples of what would be regarded as exceptional which included adultery within a few weeks of the marriage or homosexuality. However in *C.* v. *C.* (1979) the Court of Appeal considered that the concept of depravity "had fallen out of general use" and that it should not be necessary to rely on this concept any more. The court also seemed to consider that merely having to wait three years for a divorce in circumstances where the marriage had clearly broken down could itself amount to exceptional hardship. The facts of *C.* v. *C.* were that the husband, within a few weeks of the marriage, lost interest in his wife and formed a homosexual relationship. The wife could show little in the way of hardship to herself except for some loss of weight. It was held that the wife had established exceptional hardship to herself and could therefore petition for divorce within three years, but that she had not established exceptional depravity on the part of the husband.

Most of these applications are unopposed and the applicant's evidence is given by affidavit. In any case the allegations made by an applicant are not tried at this stage. "All that the court can do is to come to a conclusion that the allegations made in the affidavits filed on the application are such that, if true, they would amount to exceptional hardship or depravity" (*Winter* (1944), *per* Lord Goddard). Nevertheless the court is not bound to accept the evidence of an applicant because it is uncontradicted; and if any evidence is produced in opposition, it is taken into account in considering the probability of the truth of the applicant's complaints.

If there has been deception on the application, success may be short-lived, as a court may dismiss the petition, or grant a decree on condition that it is not to be made absolute until three years after the marriage, if it appears at the trial that leave to present a petition within three years was obtained by misrepresentation or conceal-ment (Matrimonial Causes Act 1973, s.3(3)).

2. The basic ground for divorce

Before the commencement of the Divorce Reform Act 1969 on January 1, 1971, the principal grounds for divorce were adultery, desertion for at least three years immediately preceding a petition and cruelty. In other words, the English law was based on the principle that a divorce would be granted only where the respondent had committed a matrimonial offence.

Since that date the irretrievable breakdown of a marriage has become the sole ground for dissolving it. In the words of the statute itself (s.1) " . . . the sole ground on which a petition for divorce may be presented to the court by either party to a marriage shall be that the marriage has broken down irretrievably." The provisions of the Divorce Reform Act have now been consolidated with other matrimonial matters and re-enacted in the Matrimonial Causes Act 1973.

3. Proof of the ground for divorce

The irretrievable breakdown of a marriage can only be established by proving any one or more of five facts prescribed by section 1 of the Act of 1973. Proof of any of these facts establishes the breakdown of a marriage unless the court is satisfied, looking at the evidence as a whole, that the marriage has not broken down irretrievably (Act of 1973, s.1(4)). Unless the court is satisfied of such breakdown it cannot grant a divorce. The five prescribed facts are:

(a) *That the respondent has committed adultery and the petitioner finds it intolerable to live with the respondent*

There are two elements to this fact. First, the commission of at least one act of adultery by the respondent, and secondly, that the petitioner finds life with the respondent intolerable.

(i) Meaning of adultery. Adultery is definable as voluntary sexual intercourse between two persons of whom one or both are married although not to one another. Full penetration is not necessary for an act of adultery to have taken place but there must be at least partial penetration of the woman's vagina by the man's penis (*Dennis* (1955)). Adultery is, therefore, not committed unless there is some degree of union between a man and a woman, and masturbation or a wholly abortive attempt at sexual intercourse do not constitute adultery (*Sapsford* (1954)).

As adultery must be voluntary, the rape of a wife does not amount to adultery, though she must satisfy the court that she did not consent to the act of sexual intercourse (*Redpath* (1950)) In theory where a spouse was so drugged or drunk at the time of the act that he or she could not be said to have consented, that also will be a good defence to a charge of adultery. There are no clear cases on this however.

Proof of adultery, provided that sufficient details of time, place and the other person are given in the petition and accompanying affidavits, does not usually present any difficulty as it will in any case rarely be denied. If the allegation is contested then adultery must be proved in the usual way to the civil standard of proof—the balance of probability (*Bastable* (1968)). It is no longer necessary to prove adultery "beyond all reasonable doubt." Adultery is usually inferred from evidence of affection between the couple and from the fact that they have stayed together in the same house for certain periods, especially overnight.

(ii) Intolerability. The commission of adultery by itself is insufficient to prove breakdown of marriage. The petitioner must also prove that he finds life with the respondent intolerable. Must the adultery be the *cause* of the intolerability? The courts have disagreed on this. In *Goodrich* (1971) it was held that the petitioner need not prove he found life with the responent intolerable as a result of the adultery. Thus a husband who had attempted a reconciliation with his adulterous wife obtained a divorce when that reconciliation attempt failed despite the fact that at the time of the attempt he was obviously able to contemplate living with an adulterous wife. However, in *Roper* (1972) it was held that the petitioner must find life with the respondent intolerable *in consequence* of the adultery and the judge refused to follow the decision in *Goodrich*. The Court of Appeal have held, in *Cleary* (1974), that it is not necessary to prove that the intolerability was caused by the adultery and this has been followed in the same court by *Carr* (1974), although the court was unhappy about this rule in the latter case and hoped that the House of Lords might soon consider the matter but it has not done so. The need to prove intolerability is intended, if possible, to prevent a divorce after one of the parties has committed adultery unless this lapse has really resulted in the breakdown of the marriage. This intention of the Act is emphasised by the provision that a petitioner cannot rely on the respondent's adultery as proof of breakdown if, after it has come to the knowledge of the petitioner that the respondent has committed adultery, "they have lived with each other in the same household" for a total period exceeding six months (Act of 1973, s.2(1)). On the other hand continuation or resumption of life together in one household for a period of time totalling less than six months is disregarded in considering whether a petitioner

finds it intolerable to live with the respondent (*ibid.*). An aggrieved party has therefore up to six months to decide whether or not to petition for divorce on the basis of adultery without the fear of being barred from relief should the attempt to save the marriage fail. After six months the adultery can no longer be relied on as a basis for a petition. However this bar only applies to the adultery that took place before the six months' cohabitation. In *Carr* (1974) the wife lived with the husband for over six months after she knew of his adultery with a particular woman. He then left the home and continued to commit adultery with the same woman. The wife was entitled to rely on the adultery that took place after the separation. Subject to this automatic bar, it is a question of fact in each case whether at the time of proceedings for a divorce a petitioner finds it intolerable to live with the respondent.

(b) *That the respondent has behaved in such a way that the petitioner cannot reasonably be expected to live with the respondent*

There is no limit or restriction in the Act on the kind of conduct by a respondent which might fall within the scope of this basis for proving matrimonial breakdown. On the other hand the alleged misbehaviour must clearly be "grave and weighty" in character and degree and exceed in gravity what is commonly considered "the wear and tear of married life." Thus the test used is similar to that used by their Lordships in the old cases on cruelty, *Gollins* (1963) and *Williams* (1963). Subject to this requirement it appears that the respondent's alleged behaviour must be tested in relation to the petitioner and not in relation to a reasonable man or woman (*O'Neill* (1975). The question in each case is whether the actual petitioner and not a reasonable petitioner could reasonably be expected to live with the respondent. However, there must be some breach of the obligations of married life which caused the petitioner to find life with the respondent unbearable. In *Pheasant* (1972) the husband left the wife because he considered that she had not given him the spontaneous and demonstrative affection for which his nature craved, and therefore he found it impossible to live with her any more. He failed to get a decree, the court holding that the wife had done nothing to cause the break-up of the marriage and had not committed any breach of obligation by ordinary standards. It has been said that a drunken or violent petitioner could be expected to live with a drunken or violent respondent. A spouse might be required to make allowances for a sick partner that would not be made in favour of one who was not sick (see *Katz* (1972) and *Richards* (1972)), but nevertheless, if the behaviour of the sick spouse is more than the other should reasonably be expected to endure a divorce will be granted on the basis of section 1(2)(*b*). In *Thurlow* (1975) a husband obtained a decree against a wife whose epilepsy and neurological illness prevented her from doing any work and made her incontinent and abusive. Proof of injury to the petitioner's health arising from the respondent's behaviour is not necessary, but if such proof is given to the court a petitioner can plainly not be expected to continue to live with the respondent. The same applies to an intention by a respondent to inflict misery on a petitioner. It is not necessary to prove that the respondent intended to make the life of the petitioner miserable. But if the evidence shows that it exists, no petitioner could reasonably be expected to go on living with the respondent.

How far can the other conditions upon which a divorce decree can be based also be used as evidence of behaviour under section 1(2)(*b*)? For example, could a petitioner plead adultery as evidence of behaviour? A petitioner might wish to do this because cohabitation of more than six months after the adultery is, as has been seen, an absolute bar to reliance on that adultery, but such cohabitation is not an absolute bar to a degree based on section 1(2)(*b*). An old case (*Chalcroft* (1969)) suggests that this might be acceptable. However, in a more recent case, *Stringfellow* (1976), in which the petitioner wished to plead desertion as evidence of behaviour in order to avoid having to wait for the necessary two years to elapse before petitioning on that basis, the court refused a decree on the ground that, wide though section 1(2)(*b*) was, it could not cover other conduct which the statute specified as alternative conditions for divorce.

The fact that a petitioner and respondent have continued to live together as one household for a period or periods not exceeding six months after the occurrence of the final incident relied on by a petitioner must be disregarded by the court in determining whether the petitioner cannot reasonably be expected to live with the respondent (Act of 1973, s.2(3)). More than six months' cohabitation is obviously *evidence* that the petitioner can in fact live with the respondent, but it is not *proof* of that fact and the court could therefore grant a decree despite such cohabitation.

(c) *That the respondent has deserted the petitioner for a continuous period of at least two years immediately preceding the presentation of the petition*

Desertion for a continuous period of three years immediately before the presentation of a petition was a ground for divorce until the coming into operation of the Act of 1969. Since then, desertion for a continuous period of two years is evidence of the breakdown of a marriage. For this purpose a period of desertion is not interrupted by a resumption of married life in the same household for either one period not exceeding six months or several periods not exceeding six months in all, but any period during which the parties resumed married life does not count as part of the minimum period of two years' desertion which must have existed before the commencement of the proceedings (*ibid.* s.2(5)).

(i) Elements of desertion. Desertion is the separation between husband and wife which is not mutually agreed but is occasioned by the deserter without reasonable cause and with the intention of remaining permanently apart. There are four essential elements of desertion:

(a) *The separation.* There can be no desertion on either side as long as the parties to a marriage continue to live together. It is, however, possible for a state of desertion to exist while they are still living under the same roof, provided there is no common life whatever between them. In *Hope's* case (1949) sexual relations had ceased, the wife had withdrawn into a separate bedroom and she did no washing, mending or separate cooking for her husband. On the other hand, he joined the family for most meals which were prepared by the wife and, when not in his room, he shared the rest of the house with his wife and daughters. On these facts it was held that the parties were living as one household and the husband's complaint of desertion against the wife therefore failed; but, as the following quotation from Lord Justice Denning's judgment shows, he might have succeeded if he and his wife had been living not as one but as two households:

> "One of the essential elements of desertion is the fact of separation. Can that exist while the parties are living under the same roof? My answer is 'Yes.' The husband who shuts himself up in one or two rooms of his house and ceases to have anything to do with his wife is living separately and apart from her as effectively as if they were separated by the outer door of a flat. They may meet on the stairs or in the passageway, but so they might if they each had separate flats in one building. If that separation is brought about by his fault, why is that not desertion? He has forsaken and abandoned his wife as effectively as if he had gone into lodgings. The converse is equally true. If the wife ceases to have anything to do with, or for, the husband, and he is left to look after himself in his own rooms, why is not that desertion? She has forsaken and abandoned him as effectively as if she had gone to live with her relatives . . . "

For the purpose of proof of this ingredient of desertion it does not matter whether an existing state of separation is voluntary or has been forced upon the parties by, for example, the imprisonment of either (*Beeken* (1948)).

(b) *Lack of consent*. If a husband and wife agree to live apart neither is in desertion. If this is the case divorce may be obtainable on one of the separation grounds, of course. However if for some reason the respondent will not agree to a divorce after two years separation, the petitioner will have to wait for five years before being able to petition. He or she will not have to wait this long if it can be shown that the separation was not, or is not now, consensual. It is therefore still important to be clear on what the law means by "consensual separation." It is also still relevant to the law in the magistrates' courts where desertion in a ground for an application for a matrimonial order (see p.55).

To accept without protest the other parties withdrawal from married life does not necessarily constitute conent to it. As was said in *Harriman* (1909): "Desertion does not necessarily involve that a wife desires her husband to remain with her. She may be thankful that he has gone, but he may nevertheless have deserted her." Acceptance of maintenance is similarly not inconsistent with an allegation of desertion. A spouse who has been or is about to be deserted is entitled to ask for and agree to maintenance from the deserter without thereby agreeing to the separation.

When the parties have entered into a written agreement to separate there is clear consent unless one of them was coerced into signing (*Adamson* (1907)). In the absence of a written agreement consent must be inferred from the words or conduct of the parties (*Joseph* (1953)). Consent to separation may terminate, as where a separation agreement is treated as a "dead letter" by both parties and one of them wishes to resume married life but is refused by the other (*Pardy* (1939)).

(c) *That the parties to the marriage have lived apart continuously for at least two years immediately preceding the presentation of the petition and that the respondent consents to a decree being granted.* Two elements are involved here, first, the necessary period of living apart and, secondly, the respondent's consent.

The parties to a marriage live apart if they either live in different homes or they live under the same roof but in such circumstances that there is no common life whatever between them. (For cases on the meaning of this phrase, see p.69). As the Act of 1973 itself put it in section 2(6): " . . . a husband and wife shall be treated as living apart unless they are living with each other in the same household."

The parties may be living apart for a number of reasons ranging from genuine matrimonial estrangement to the demands of business, or because one spouse is in hospital or prison. Will they be held to be living apart under this provision whatever the reason for their separation? In *Santos* (1972) it was decided that if, although they were living apart, both spouses recognised that their matrimonial life together still subsisted, then they would be unable to rely on such a separation for the purposes of getting a divorce under section 1(2)(*d*). Thus, for example, if a husband has been in prison for two years, his wife would only be able to get a divorce on the grounds of separation only if for the whole of that two years either she or her husband had made up their minds that the marriage was at an end. The court in *Santos* did not think it was necessary for one spouse to tell the other of his intentions.

With regard to the requirement of continuity for two years the position is the same as for desertion. Accordingly a period during which parties are living apart is not interrupted by a resumption of married life in the same household for one or more periods totalling less than six months, but such period or periods do not count as part of the period of living apart (Act of 1973, s.2(5)).

Whether the respondent consents to the grant of a decree of divorce is a question of fact in each case. In order to ensure that any consent has been given by a respondent with full understanding of its implications, rules under the Act of 1973 require that the respondent shall be given "such information as will enable him to understand the consequences to him of his consenting to a decree being granted and the steps which he must take to indicate that he consents to the grant of decree" (*ibid.* s.2(7).) In general, consent is indicated by sending a signed notice to this effect to the Registrar (*Matcham* 1976). An insane spouse can validly consent only if he is capable of understanding the nature and effect of his action (*Mason* (1972)). A respondent who has been misled by a petitioner about any matter which the respondent took into account in deciding to consent to the grant of a decree may at any time between decree nisi and decree absolute apply to the court for the decree nisi to be rescinded. Such an application may succeed if the court is satisfied that the petitioner, whether intentionally or unintentionally, misled the respondent about any matter which influenced the respondent in giving his consent (*ibid.* s.10(1)).

(d) *That the parties to the marriage have lived apart for a continuous period of at least five years immediately preceding the presentation of the petition*
   The difference between this fact and the preceding fact is two-fold. The length of the period of separation is five years instead of two,

and the respondent's consent or opposition to the granting of a decree is irrelevant. Irrespective, therefore, of a respondent's wishes or attitude, the mere proof of a five years' continuous separation between parties to a marriage immediately before the commencement of proceedings is capable of proving the breakdown of the marriage and will do so unless the evidence as a whole does not satisfy the court that despite such separation the marriage has irretrievably broken down.

4. Defences to the grant of a decree nisi

The fact that a petition is undefended does not mean that it will necessarily succeed, as even the uncontradicted evidence of the petitioner and of any other witnesses may not satisfy the court that any of the five facts from which the breakdown of a marriage can be inferred has been proved or that, notwithstanding such proof, a marriage has broken down irretrievably. A court is always concerned with truth, and its duty to search for it is emphasised by section 1 (3) of the Act of 1973 which provides that: "On a petition for divorce it shall be the duty of the court to inquire, so far as it reasonably can, into the facts alleged by the petitioner and into any facts alleged by the respondent.

A respondent who wishes to defend a petition may do so by denying whatever facts the petitioner seeks to prove to show the irretrievable breakdown of the marriage or by contending that, although the facts alleged by the petitioner are admitted, the marriage has nevertheless not broken down irretrievably. For example, in answer to a husband's petition alleging adultery by his wife and that he finds it intolerable to live with her, she may deny being guilty of adultery or that her husband finds it intolerable to live with her or both these facts. Alternatively she may argue that despite her adultery and her husband's attitude to her the marriage has not irretrievably broken down. A further alternative open to her is to countercharge in the same proceedings by alleging against her husband any of the facts which are capable of proving the breakdown of their marriage (Matrimonial Causes Act 1973, s.20).

Grave financial or other hardship

A special defence is available to a respondent in a case where the petitioner relies on the fact of five years' separation for proof of the irretrievable breakdown of the marriage. The defence is provided by section 5 of the Act of 1973 and enables a respondent to oppose the grant of a decree nisi "on the ground that the dissolution of the marriage will result in grave financial or other hardship to him and that it would in all the circumstances be wrong to dissolve the marriage . . . ." This defence can succeed and lead to the dismissal of a petition only if, after hearing the evidence and arguments, "the court is of opinion that the dissolution of the marriage will result in grave financial or other hardsip to the respondent (including the loss of the chance of acquiring any benefit which the respondent might acquire if the marriage were not dissolved) and that it would be wrong in all the circumstances to dissolve the marriage."

This defence, therefore, requires proof of two distinct elements. First, grave financial or other grave hardship to the respondent if the marriage were dissolved and, secondly, facts and matters which in the opinion of the court would in all the circumstances make it wrong to dissolve the marriage. In considering both these elements the court is expressly directed by the same section of the Act to "consider all the circumstances, including the conduct of the parties to the marriage and the interests of these parties and of any children or other persons concerned."

With regard to the first element it is only "grave" hardship which satisfies the ingredient of this defence. Ordinary hardship does not qualify. It must be exceptional and out of the ordinary. The respondent must also prove that the alleged hardship will be a consequence of the *divorce* and not simply a consequence of the spouse's separation. (*Talbot* (1971)). In view of the court's wide powers to make financial orders and transfer property on divorce, this will be a difficult matter to prove. The most obvious hardship to a wife which is also clearly a consequence of divorce is the loss of the expectation of a widow's pension. In *Parker* (1972) the couple were in middle age and had been married for about 20 years. The husband, a policeman, had left the wife for another woman and, after five years had elapsed, petitioned for a divorce. The wife alleged that a divorce would cause her grave financial hardship because she would lose her right to a police widow's pension. It was held that in all the circumstances this was grave financial hardship but the husband was able to compensate adequately for this by purchasing a deferred annuity in her favour, so the divorce was granted. In *Mathias* (1972) the couple had lived together for only two years and then the husband, a soldier, had left the wife for another woman. After eight years' separation he petitioned for a divorce on the grounds of five years' separation and the wife opposed it on the grounds of grave financial hardship. She had one child. On divorce she alleged that she would lose the security of army maintenance, that the husband would re-marry and thus her maintenance would be reduced, and that she would lose the right to an army and state widow's pension. It was held that although there was some financial hardship, it was not grave. The wife was young and her financial problems were partly caused by her own decision not to work but to devote herself to looking after the child. Her prospect of a widow's pension was remote. The court also had to consider the broader aspects of the case which was that the marriage had hopelessly broken down and that all three of the parties involved had many years ahead of them and all might desire to marry again. It has been held to be no grave hardship if the loss of a pension would be adequately compensated for by supplementary benefit. In *Reiterbund* (1975) a wife aged 52 opposed the divorce on the ground that if her divorced husband were to die before she reached 60 (when she would be entitled to a retirement pension) she would lose her entitlement to a widow's pension. However she would be entitled, in such an event, to apply for a similar amount in supplementary benefit and the court did not consider that the supposed "shame" of applying for supplementary benefit was a grave hardship.

Hardship other than financial hardship is even more difficult to establish. Religious objections to divorce are not usually sufficient (*Rukat* (1975)), but such objections might usually succeed if allied to evidence that a divorce would result in social ostracism and disgrace for the respondent wife, as for example where the couple were living in a traditional Hindu community (*Banik* (1973).

On the second element of the defence, that it would be, in all the circumstances, wrong to dissolve the marriage, there is little guidance. It is clear, however, that conduct is relevant. In *Brickell* (1974) the loss to a wife of a pension was held to be grave hardship but the husband obtained his divorce because of the wife's disgraceful conduct towards him.

5. Restrictions on the grant of a decree absolute

There are two such restrictions. The first one existed before the enactment of the Divorce Reform Act 1969 and survives it in amended form (Matrimonial Causes Act 1973, s.41). It prohibits the making absolute of a decree of divorce or nullity of marriage or the making of a decree of judicial separation unless the court has by order declared either that there are no children of the family or, if there are or may be such children, that the arrangements for their custody, education and financial provision are either satisfactory or are the best that can be devised in the circumstances or that it is impracticable for the party or parties appearing before the court to make any such arrangements.

This restriction applies to any child of the family (see p.95) who at the date of the order is under the age of 16 or such a child of any age who is "receiving instruction at an educational establishment or undergoing training for a trade, profession or vocation, whether or not he is also in gainful employment." The court may in special circumstances extend the scope of the restriction to any other child if of the opinion that such course is desirable in his interest.

A decree absolute or a decree of judicial separation made without a declaratory order regarding the arrangements for any children of the family of their non-existence is legally void. The purpose of this restriction and of the detailed provisions relating to it is to ensure that there is no divorce, annulment or judicial separation without the welfare of the children concerned having first been considered and protected as far as possible. In very exceptional circumstances the court may lift the restriction, provided it has received satisfactory undertakings from either or both parties to bring the question of the arrangements for the children before the court within a specified time.

The second restriction rests on section 10(2)–(4) of the 1973 Act and concerns the financial protection of a respondent. It applies only if a decree nisi has been pronounced on a petition between the parties and that respondent has applied to the court to consider the financial position of the respondent after the divorce. Subsection (3) prohibits the making absolute of a decree nisi unless the court is satisfied that:

"(a) the petitioner should not be required to make any financial provision for the respondent,or
 (b) the financial provision made by the petitioner for the respondent is reasonable and fair or the best that can be made in the circumstances," or
 "it appears that there are circumstances making it desirable that the decree should be made absolute without delay, and the court has obtained a satisfctory undertaking from the petitioner that he will make such financial provision for the respondent as the court may approve"(*ibid.* subs.(4)).

On hearing such application by a respondent the court must consider "all the circumstances, including the age, health, conduct, earning capacity, financial resources and financial obligations of each of the parties, and the financial position of the respondent as, having regard to the divorce, it is likely to be after the death of the petitioner should the petitioner die first." Failure to comply with these provisions renders the decree absolute voidable, not void, according to the decision in *Wright* (1976). In order to save unnecessary expense or delay, either party may apply to the court before or at any time after the presentation of a petition for an expression of opinion on the reasonableness of any agreement or arrangement made or proposed to be made between the parties (Act of 1973, s.7).

6. Practice and procedure

As has already been noted the overwhelming majority of divorce cases are undefended. They are therefore dealt with in the county court under a procedure that is still known as the "special procedure" but which is, in fact, the normal or usual procedure. This procedure, which makes the granting of a divorce decree an almost entirely administrative process, was introduced by rules of the county court and is not to be found in any statute. It was introduced mainly in order to reduce the amount of money spent on legal aid for divorce by allowing litigants to conduct their own cases, without the need for a solicitor's help. Legal aid is still available in the usual way for contested ancillary proceedings such as maintenance and custody.

The first step is for the petitioner to fill in and file a petition for divorce in the relevant county court. The petition must be accompanied by a "statement of arrangements" form, which sets out what arrangements have been and are to be made for any children of the family. These documents, which are fairly simple but with which many will welcome expert advice in filling them in, are served by the court on the respondent. Forms explain to the respondent how to acknowledge service, how to consent and to indicate whether or not he wishes to defend the action. Where the case is not defended and any necessary consents have been given the special procedure can continue.

The petitioner asks for the case to be put on the special procedure list and files an affidavit (sworn statement) of evidence supporting the petition in the required form. The registrar then considers all the documents and, if satisfied that all is in order and that a decree ought to be granted, he gives a certificate to that effect. A decree nisi can then be granted by a judge in the county court. This is a purely formal step and the parties do not have to be present and neither are they orally examined on the allegations made in the petition. Once the registrar has issued his certificate the decree nisi must be pronounced unless the respondent gets leave to set the certificate aside, which will be granted if justice demands that he be given leave to defend (*Day* (1980)).

The above is a brief account of the procedure which is described in more detail for the benefit of litigants in person in a booklet issued by the Lord Chancellor's Office and available, with the appropriate forms, from the county court office.

If the case is to be defended, the respondent must file an answer after receiving the petition. The case is then transferred to the High Court for a full hearing and all the normal steps in a civil action will be gone through.

In both defended and undefended cases a minimum period of six weeks must elapse between the granting of a decree nisi and a decree absolute, which finally dissolves the marriage. A shorter period may be applied for and will be granted if there are good reasons for it, *e.g.* to allow an expected child to be born legitimate. An application for a decree absolute will normally be made by the successful petitioner but if he delays doing this for more than six weeks after being entitled to apply then the respondent may apply for the decree absolute (1973 Act, s.9(2)). There is no further hearing for the grant of the final decree. The decree may however be refused if an appeal is pending, if arrangements have not been made for the children or if the respondent was misled in some way when he gave his consent to a divorce on the basis of separation. Section 10(1) of the 1973 Act provides that a decree nisi may be rescinded if the petitioner misled the respondent on any matter which he took into account when giving consent.

B. Judicial Separation

The effect of a decree of judicial separation is to release the spouses from their duty to cohabit without dissolving the marriage. Decrees are comparatively rare and generally sought by those with religious objections to divorce or by those who have no ground for divorce, *e.g.* where the two or five years of separation has not been established. Such petitioners may well want the protection of the court in property matters, especially in relation to the matrimonial home, which is available when the court makes a decree of judicial separation.

There is no restriction on instituting proceedings for judicial separation within the first three years of marriage. A petition for judicial separation can be brought at any time after the celebration of a marriage without the leave of the court. The grounds for a decree of judicial separation are the existence of any of the five facts which are capable of proving the irretrievable breakdown of amarriage in proceedings for divorce. These five prescribed facts are, as we have seen, set out in section 1 of the Matrimonial Causes Act 1973 and are dealt with earlier in this chapter (see p.65). For the purpose of proceedings for judicial separation it does not matter whether a marriage has irretrievably broken down as a result of any of these facts, and the court is not concerned to consider this question (Matrimonial Causes Act 1973, s.17(2)).

The only defence open to a respondent to a petition for judicial separation is a denial of whichever of the five facts is alleged in the petition. On proof of any one of these the court must grant a decree subject to the requirements of section 41 of the Matrimonial Causes Act 1973 regarding the arrangements for any child to which this section applied (*ibid.* s.17(2)).

English courts have jurisdiction to entertain proceedings for judicial separation in the same circumstances as they can entertain divorce proceedings.

The practice and procedure relating to petitions for judicial separation and the court's incidental powers are the same as for petitions for divorce except that a successful petition for judicial separation results in an immediately effective decree and not in a decree nisi which is made absolute at a later date.

CHAPTER 7

NULLITY

The distinction between void and voidable marriage is vital to an understanding of the law of nullity. A "void marriage" is really a contradiction in terms, as such a marriage has from its beginning no existence or validity whatever in the eyes of the law. A "voidable marriage" on the other hand, is and remains a valid marriage until a court annuls it by pronouncing a decree of nullity on the application of either party to the marriage. The distinction was described by Lord Greene M.R. in *De Reneville's* case (1948) as follows

> "A void marriage is one that will be regarded by every court in any case in which the existence of the marriage is an issue as never having taken place and can be so treated by both parties to it without the necessity of any decree annulling it; a voidable marriage is one that will be regarded by every court as a valid subsisting marriage until a decree annulling it has been pronounced by a court of competent jurisdiction."

In theory, a decree annulling a voidable marriage used to be treated as operating retrospectively, but it has been made clear by the Nullity of Marriage Act 1971, s.5 (now the Matrimonial Causes Act 1973, s.16), that such a marriage is annulled only from the date of the decree. This Act consolidated the law relating to nullity and also made some changes. Its provisions are now contained in the Matrimonial Causes Act 1973, ss.11–16. The Act only applies to marriages celebrated since it came into force on August 1, 1971, and therefore the courts might still have to deal with cases under the old law. In order to avoid complication, the account of the law outlined below is confined to the law under the Act. Comparatively few nullity cases come before the courts each year. In 1980 there were 1,110 petitions filed for nullity, as compared with 177,415 petitions for divorce.

A. VOID MARRIAGE

A marriage whose validity depends on English law, and which takes place after August 1, 1971, is void if:

1. Either party was under the age of 16 at the time of the ceremony (see p.4).
2. The parties are within the prohibited degrees of consanguinity or affinity (see p.5).

3. Either party was already lawfully married at the time of the ceremony (Matrimonial Causes Act 1973, s.11(*b*)) (see p.6).
4. It was knowingly celebrated without some of the essential formalities (see p.00).
5. The parties are not respectively male and female (Matrimonial Causes Act 1973, s.11(*c*), and see also *Corbett* (1971) and p.4).
6. The marriage was celebrated abroad and is polygamous, either party being domiciled in England and Wales at the time of its celebration (Matrimonial Causes Act 1973, s.11(*d*)) (see p.12)

If a marriage is void for any of these reasons, it is, as Lord Greene points out, not necessary for the parties to obtain a declaration of nullity from a court, as the marriage is of no legal effect without a formal judicial pronouncement, and the parties can treat it as such without resort to a court. Although this course is, no doubt, adopted from time to time, a formal declaration of nullity is usually sought, as generally the invalidity of a marriage is not agreed between the parties, or the facts relevant to its validity are in dispute, or the legal questions involved are difficult and capable of more than one answer. In any event a declaratory decree of nullity is the best possible evidence for all concerned that the marriage in question is void. Resort to a court has the further advantage of making available to the parties the court's jurisdiction of making appropriate orders for financial relief and in respect of any children (Matrimonial Causes Act 1973, ss.21–24).

B. Voidable Marriages

Grounds for annulment

A marriage celebrated since August 1, 1971, is voidable on the following grounds:

(a) *That either party to the marriage is incapable of consummating the marriage due to impotence and the marriage has not been consummated.*

Impotence may be due to physiological causes and may be an inability to have sexual intercourse with all persons of the opposite sex or merely with the other party to the marriage. For the purpose of annulment all these varieties of inability constitute impotence provided it is proved to have existed throughout the marriage and there is no "practical possibility of consummation" at the time of the hearing of the petition. No such possibility exists if at that time the afflicted party probably cannot be cured, or refuses to undergo an operation which is not dangerous and likely to cure, or the inability can be cured only by an operation attended by danger (*S. v. S. orse. C.* (1963)).

An impotent husband or wife may himself petition for a decree of nullity, and on proof of his impotence is entitled to a decree unless the petitioner was aware of his impotence at the time of his marriage (*Harthan* (1949)) or if the petitioner was ignorant of his inability, it is in all the circumstances held to be unjust and unfair that the impotent party should be granted a decree on his own application. In *Pettit's* case (1963) the Court of Appeal on this ground refused a decree to an impotent husband who left his wife after 20 years when he fell in love with another woman. He only then discovered that his own impotence enabled him to petition for the annulment of his marriage. The factors which were held to make it unjust in the case to grant him a decree were the long period of cohabitation of the parties, the wife's age of 53 at the time of the petition, her forbearance and acceptance of her husband without reproach for so many years, the position of their daughter who was then in her teens and had been conceived by fertilisation from outside the wife, and the wife's loss of status and rights as a widow if her husband predeceased her.

(b) *That the marriage has not been consummated owing to the wilful refusal of the respondent to consummate it*

This and the following grounds for the annulment of a marriage became part of English law only by the enactment of the Matrimonial Causes Act 1937 which was introduced and piloted through Parliament by Mr. A. P. Herbert, M.P. (see now the Matrimonial Causes Act 1973, s.12(*b*)). "Wilful refusal" as this ground is known for short requires, first of all, proof that a marriage has not been consummated. Legally a marriage is consummated if the parties have, on at least one occasion, engaged in an act of sexual intercourse during which the husband fully penetrated his wife for an appreciable moment. Partial and imperfect sexual play or union short of full penetration does not amount to consummation.

In *Baxter's* case (1948) the House of Lords rejected the argument of a husband that his marriage had not been consummated as, owing to his wife's insistence, he had always worn a contraceptive sheath during sexual intercourse thereby preventing the possibility of conception. Lord Jowitt explained the dismissal of the husband's petition in the following words:

> "In any view of Christian marriage the essence of the matter . . . is that the children, if there be any, should be born

into a family, as that word is understood in Christendom generally . . . but this is not the same thing as saying that a marriage is not consummated unless children are procreated or that procreation of children is the principal end of marriage."

Proof of non-consummation alone is not sufficient for the annulment of a marriage on this ground. It must further be proved that the non-consummation was due to the respondent's wilful refusal. This is established by evidence that the petitioner proposed sexual intercourse to the respondent "with such tact, persuasion and encouragement as an ordinary husband (or wife) would use in the circumstances" and that the respondent refused intercourse by behaviour displaying "a settled and definite decision come to without just excuse." The refusal can be implied, as illustrated by *Jodla's* case (1960), in which a wife petitioned for the annulment of her marriage celebrated in a register office. The parties were Poles of Roman Catholic persuasion and they had mutually agreed that the civil wedding should be followed by a religious ceremony. After the wedding, however, the husband refused to make arrangements for such further ceremony although he knew that his wife was willing to have sexual intercourse with him only after such solemnisation. He in fact showed no interest in sexual intercourse and it never took place. On these facts the court held that the husband's failure to arrange a religious wedding implied a refusal on his part to consummate the marriage and his wife's petition accordingly succeeded. There must be an intention to refuse intercourse on the part of the respondent. Mere "loss of ardour" for the petitioner is not sufficient (*Potter* (1975)).

(c) *That either party to the marriage did not validly consent to it because of duress, mistake, unsoundness of mind, "or otherwise"* (Matrimonial Causes Act 1973, s.12(c))

Until 1971 these matters rendered a marriage void. Now the marriage will be voidable but the old law concerning the nature of duress and mistake, etc., will still apply.

(i) Duress. Fear or duress may invalidate the consent of either party to the marriage and so make it voidable.

In *Cooper* v. *Crane* (1891) this principle was unsuccessfully invoked by a wealthy young woman of 27 who for good reasons regretted her marriage to her "wicked and determined" cousin aged 20. According to her evidence they were on their way to a service at St. Pauls's one Sunday morning when, passing St. Bride's church—where unknown to her he had made arrangements for a wedding—he confronted her with a sudden and totally unexpected proposal of marriage in these words: "You must come into the church and marry me or I will blow out my brains and you will be responsible." She claimed to have been so terrified by this threat which she considered to be genuine that she did not afterwards know what she was doing. Unfortunately for her the vicar's recollection was that she showed no sign of nerves or unwillingness during the ceremony, repeated her responses in "audible tones" and signed the register in a "clear and firm hand." It was agreed that after the ceremony the young man took her home, where he left her at the door, and that they never lived as husband and wife. In correspondence he later admitted to having married his cousin for money and without caring for her. In refusing the woman a declaration that her consent to the marriage was not freely given due to fear, the judge stated it to be "clear law" that if she did not in fact consent to the marriage the court will declare it null. On the other hand, when a person of full age and of sound mind has gone through the ceremony of marriage publicly in the presence of witnesses who discovered nothing in her demeanour to suggest constraint, and has herself complied with the formality of signing her name and answering questions without apparent difficulty or confusion, very clear and cogent evidence must be given before the presumption of consent can be rebutted . . . "

Recent cases have emphasised that there must exist a reasonably entertained fear of a threat to life, limb or liberty (*Szechter* (1971)). To acquiesce to an arranged marriage so as not to incur parental anger will not constitute duress (*Singh* (1971)). Moreover in *Buckland* (1968) it was pointed out by the judge that if the petitioner was himself responsible for the circumstances that gave rise to his fears, his consent to his marriage would not be held to be vitiated. In that case a British policeman serving in Malta took out a Maltese girl aged 15. Nothing improper occurred between them but her father charged the petitioner with "minor corruption," an offence which carried a heavy prison sentence. The petitioner was told that such was the feeling against British serving personnel that there was little chance of his being acquitted. In order to avoid the charge he therefore married the girl. The marriage was never consummated and he soon returned to England alone. The marriage was annulled for duress. Had he in fact committed the offence no decree would have been granted, though it might well be thought that his fears would have been even greater in that event and that therefore his consent to the marriage even less likely to have been voluntarily given.

(ii) Mistake. Mistake will rarely make a marriage voidable. To do so the mistake must be really fundamental, so that the petitioner either mistakes the nature of the ceremony he is involved in or is mistaken as to the identity of the person he is marrying. Being mistaken as to some attribute of the respondent, such as his wealth or health, is not enough. A case where mistake did cause the marriage to be annulled is that of *Valier* (1925) where the petitioner was a rather simple Italian with little knowledge of English who thought that the marriage ceremony he had been through was merely one of betrothal.

(iii) Unsoundness of mind. The question to be answered here is what degree of insanity is necessary to vitiate the consent of the petitioner to the ceremony? This is the matter which concerned the court in *In the Estate of Park* (1954) which resulted from the remarriage of a widower aged 78 who made a will in favour of his second wife on the wedding day of his marriage to her. On that day, due to two strokes in the previous 15 months, Mr. Park, the widower, was in a very poor mental and physical condition and he in fact survived his wedding day by only 18 days.

In due course the validity of the will was contested by the members of his first family which in the ensuing litigation raised the issues of his testamentary capacity and of his mental capacity to remarry on his second wedding day, as the validity of this marriage was relevant to the distribution of his estate. In the result the court declared against the will for lack of testamentary understanding, but upheld the validity of the marriage which called for a different degree and kind of understanding, defined by the Court of Appeal as follows:

> "To ascertain the nature of the contract of marriage a person must be mentally capable of appreciating that it involves the responsibilities normally attaching to marriage. Without that degree of mentality, it cannot be said that he or she understands the nature of the contract."

Other factors which might vitiate consent are the influence of drink or drugs at the time of the ceremony, or senile decay.

(d) *That at the time of the marriage either party, though capable of giving a valid consent, was suffering from a mental disorder (either continuous or intermittent) within the Mental Health Act 1959 which makes them unfitted for marriage*

(e) *That the respondent was at the time of the marriage suffering from venereal disease in a communicable form*

The requirement that the disease must at the specified time have existed "in a communicable form" means that it must then have been infectious.

(f) *That the respondent wife was at the time of the marriage pregnant by some person other than the petitioner*

Restrictions on granting a decree of nullity

"In a suit for nullity of marriage there may be facts and circumstances provided which so plainly imply, on the part of the complaining spouse, a recognition of the existence and validity of the marriage, as to render it most inequitable and contrary to public policy that he or she should be permitted to go on to challenge it with effect." (*G.* v. *M.* (1885), *per* Lord Watson.)

This principle is now contained in the Matrimonial Causes Act 1973, s.13, which forbids the court to grant a decree where the marriage is voidable if the petitioner's conduct had led the respondent reasonably to believe he would not seek to annul the marriage and where it would be unjust to grant the decree. The principle is illustrated by the following two cases. In *W.* v. *W.* (1952) a decree of nullity was refused to a husband petitioner who before instituting proceedings had jointly with his impotent wife adopted a child with full knowledge at the time of the adoption that he was entitled to have his marriage annulled. On the other hand in *Slater* (1953) adoption was not held to be a bar to a wife's petition because, when she and her husband adopted a child, her knowledge of her rights regarding the annulment of her marriage was merely "hazy," and after she became fully aware of her rights she did nothing which could be regarded as accepting the marriage.

Mere delay does not, in the case of impotence and wilful refusal, necessarily imply acceptance of the marriage, but the longer a petition is postponed the greater the need for rebutting the inference that the delay is in fact due to this.

Other restrictions which exist apply only to a petition based on any ground other than impotence or wilful refusal. Such petitions must be commenced within three years of the celebration of the marriage. In the case of venereal disease and pregnancy by another, the petitioner must have been ignorant of these facts at the time of the marriage. A petitioner can plead ignorance only if a "reasonable man" in his shoes could have done so. The test, in other words, is objective (*Smith* (1948)).

Jurisdiction

English courts have jurisdiction to hear proceedings for a decree of nullity in all cases in which they may pronounce a decree of divorce and in the following additional circumstance. If either of the spouses died before the date when the proceedings were begun, then, if either had been domiciled or habitually resident prior to the date of death, the court has jurisdiction.

Practice and procedure

Proceedings for nullity can be started immediately after the celebration of a marriage as, unlike in divorce, there is no three years' limitation before a petition may be presented without leave. Otherwise the procedure applicable to a petition for nullity is generally the same as for a petition for a divorce. In proceedings based on impotence or wilful refusal, the services of medical inspectors are available in appropriate cases, and evidence relating to any party's sexual capacity is given *in camera* unless the court is satisfied that it ought to be heard in open court (Matrimonial Causes Act 1973, s.48(2)). The same financial relief is obtainable in proceedings for nullity as for divorce, and the court's powers concerning children are also the same (see pp. 87 and 110, *post*).

CHAPTER 8

FINANCIAL AND PROPERTY ORDERS ON MARRIAGE BREAKDOWN

It is on pronouncing a decree of divorce or judicial separation that the courts have the most far reaching powers to make orders relating to the income and other property of the spouses. The magistrates' courts also have powers to make financial orders but they can order only unsecured periodical payments or lump sum orders of up to £500. On divorce the court has power to make unlimited lump sum orders, orders relating to the ownership and occupation of the matrimonial home, property adjustment orders as well as orders for secured or unsecured maintenance. This chapter describes the extent of these powers and the principles followed by the courts in using them. The courts can exercise the same powers when granting a decree of nullity but whether or not the same principles will be followed is doubtful. There are virtually no reported cases concerning financial provision where a marriage is declared void or voidable.

1. Orders that can be made

Pending the hearing of a petition for divorce or judicial separation the court has the power to order maintenance pending suit (Matrimonial Causes Act 1973, s.22). This lasts until the decree is pronounced and is intended as temporary maintenance.

On pronouncing a decree, *or at any time thereafter*, the court may make any of the following orders in favour of *either* spouse or the children of the marriage:

(a) Periodical payments for either spouse, either secured or unsecured,
(b) Periodical payments for the children, either secured or unsecured,
(c) A lump sum for either spouse or children,
(d) An order to transfer any property in which either spouse has an interest to either spouse or the children,
(e) An order that specified property be sold (Matrimonial Homes and Property Act 1981, s.7),
(f) A settlement of property for the benefit of either spouse of the children,

 (g) A variation of an existing settlement, including an order extinguishing or reducing a spouses' interest in such settlement.

(Matrimonial Causes Act 1973, ss.23 and 24).

The court also has powers to vary some of these orders, see p.98.

Wide though these powers are, there are certain orders that the court cannot make. It cannot, for example, order a husband to take out an insurance policy to benefit the wife at some future date or to compensate her for the loss of her expectations of a pension based on his pension contributions. (*Milne* (1981)). There is no power to order a party to make payments to third parties, such as to pay school fees or mortgage installments direct. However, where an undertaking is given to the court to make such payments, the court can enforce the undertaking (*Gandolfo* (1980)).

2. Maintenance and lump sums for spouses

Maintenance may be secured or unsecured. A secured order is simply an order that one spouse pay to the other a fixed sum each week or month. Where a secured order is made property may be transferred to trustees who pay the income to the recipient of the order. Alternatively, property owned by the payer is charged with the payment of the maintenance.

A lump sum may be for any amount but only one sum may be ordered and the order cannot subsequently be varied (*Coleman* (1973)). A lump sum order may be payable all at once or it may be payable in installments. These installments can be varied.

Maintenance orders last until the death of the payer unless a shorter period is specified by the court, or until the remarriage of the payee. No order can be made if at the time of the application either of the spouses has remarried (1973 Act, s.28)).

What principles will the court take into account in making orders? The main source of guidance is section 25(1) of the 1973 Act. The court must consider:

 "all the circumstances of the case including the following matters . . .

 (a) the income, earning capacity, property and other financial resources which each of the parties to the marriage has or is likely to have in the forseeable future;

 (b) the financial needs, obligations and responsibilities which each of the parties to the marriage has or is likely to have in the foreseeable future;

 (c) the standard of living enjoyed by the family before the breakdown of the marriage;

    (d) the age of each party to the marriage and the duration of the marriage;

    (e) any physical or mental disability of either of the parties to the marriage;

    (f) the contributions made by each of the parties to the welfare of the family, including any contribution made by looking after the home or caring for the family;

    (g) in the case of proceedings for divorce or nullity of marriage, the value to either of the parties to the marriage of any benefit (for example, a pension) which, by reason of the dissolution or annulment of the marriage, that party will lose the chance of acquiring."

The court must then "place the parties, so far as it is practicable and, having regard to their conduct, just to do so, in the financial position in which they would have been if the marriage had not broken down and each had properly discharged his or her financial obligations and responsibilities towards the other." This last provision has been subjected to considerable criticism recently as it means that a spouse, generally a wife, is encouraged to expect maintenance for life after divorce. It is argued that the existence of "no fault" divorce is incompatible with the idea that an ex-spouse should have an automatic entitlement to life-long maintenance. On the other hand it is clear that in fact very few wives do enjoy such support as few ex-husbands have the resources to pay it. The Law Commission has just reported on the issue and recommends the abolition of the criteria in section 25 that the parties should be placed in the financial position in which they would have been had the marriage not broken down. It also recommends that the maintenance of children be made an overriding priority on the spouse's resources. (Law Commission Report No. 112 1981).

It is often very difficult to predict what financial order will be made in any case because each depends on its individual circumstances. Indeed in *Sharpe* (1981) Lord Justice Ormrod said that because of this, "there was no need to look at the reported cases." This is not particularly helpful to either lawyers or their clients. Despite *Sharpe* there are certain factors that will be taken into account by the courts when making a financial order. The following, which is not meant to be exhaustive, are some of the main considerations:

(a) The "one third" rule

In *Wachtel* (1973) the Court of Appeal laid down some guidelines which have subsequently been influential. The court considered that, *as a starting point*, a wife should expect to receive one third of the parties' joint capital and income (additional provision being made for the children). Therefore if a husband earned £9000 a year and his wife earned £3000, she would receive £1000 a year from him for her maintenance, making her total income £4000, which is one third of their total joint incomes. It has often been stressed that this rule is only a starting point and in a great many cases will be modified in the light of other considerations. It will rarely be appropriate where the parties are very rich or very poor and will often be modified in the light of the parties housing costs (*Furniss* (1981)). It may be modified because of the parties conduct or by the fact that one of the parties is living with and being maintained by, or maintaining, another. Much will also depend on the responsibilities of the parties to any children.

(b) *Conduct*

Under a section 25 the court must try to make an order which places the parties in the position that they would have enjoyed had the marriage continued if this is just *having regard to their conduct*. The intention behind this provision was to exclude consideration of conduct from the majority of cases, in line with the philosophy of "no fault" divorce underlying the 1969 Divorce Reform Act. The court should concentrate on needs and responsibilities rather than on guilt and innocence. This intention was not however spelled out in the legislation itself, but, in line with this philosophy, it was laid down in the case of *Wachtel* (1973) that conduct should modify financial provision only if it was "gross and obvious." By this it is meant that a party must have plainly "wilfully persisted in conduct, or a course of conduct, calculated to destroy the marriage in circumstances in which the other party is substantially blameless," (*per* Bagnall J. in *Harnett* (1973)). A wife who shot her husband (*Armstrong* (1974)) and one who refused ever to live with her husband (*West* (1978)) had their financial provision reduced because of their conduct. A husband who severely wounded his wife so that she was unable to continue her profession as a nurse was ordered to provide more than he might otherwise have been ordered to pay. (*Jones* (1976)).

(c) *Length of marriage*

Both the age of the parties and the duration of the marriage must be considered under section 25. In general the younger the wife and the shorter the marriage the less likely it is that she will get substantial financial provision as the court will tend to favour a "clean break" between the parties if there are no children (*Khan* (1980)). However if the parties have not cohabited for years, though still formally married, little or no maintenance will be ordered, as in *Krystman* (1973) where the parties had cohabited for a fortnight although married for 26 years. Pre-marital cohabitation will be taken into account, especially where there are children, as in *Kokosinski* (1980) where the duration of the marriage was short but the parties had cohabited for 25 years and had had a child. A period of unmarried cohabitation may, however, be given less weight than married cohabitation. (*Foley* 1981)).

(d) A "clean break"

It is often suggested that it would be better for the parties if the financial order made by the court created a "clean break" between them. By this is meant that there should be an equitable division of property and perhaps a lump sum order but *no* order for continuing periodical payments. Many wives would, in any case, prefer the security of a once and for all payment of a capital sum rather than have to rely on erratically paid maintenance. A clean break can only be achieved in cases where there is sufficient property to compensate a wife for the loss of her right to continuing maintenance. It is an option open only to the well-to-do. It is also inappropriate in cases where there are children to bring up which necessarily involves the non custodial spouse in paying for their maintenance (*Moore* (1980)). Even if the parties do agree to a clean break, it is always open to one of them to go back to the court for maintenance for the children (see p.52). It has also been held that a clean break cannot be achieved as between a husband and wife unless the wife *agrees* to her application for periodical payments being finally dismissed by the court (*Dipper* (1980)). The Law Commission have recommended that a wife's consent should not be essential to the making of a "clean break" order (Law Commission Report No. 112, 1981).

(e) Calculating resources and responsibilities

Obviously the amount of maintenance or lump sum that can be ordered depends upon the way the court calculates resources and allocates responsibilities. All resources, both current income, earning capacity, future and present capital, pension entitlements, overtime pay, benefits in kind, etc., will be considered.

Where either spouse is living with a new partner this will be taken into account. If the husband is supporting a new partner or children this will reduce the resources available for the support of the first wife and children. The needs of the first family must be given priority over the second (*Roberts* (1970)). Equally if a husband is being relieved of expenses by being housed or supported by his new partner this will be taken into account when assessing the amount of his resources that are available to support his first family (*Ette* (1964); *Macey* (1981)). The income of a new partner cannot however be used directly to support the first family.

A wife's income will normally be taken into account in full, and a younger wife, in particular if childless, will usually be expected to support herself (*Adams* (1978)). However, if the wife has been forced to seek work because of the breakdown of the marriage and it is not considered reasonable for her to work because she is looking after the children, she is old or she has not been expected to work for many years, then her earnings may not be taken into account in full (*Attwood* (1968)).

The court will ignore a wife's entitlement to supplementary benefit in most cases (see below) but it will take into account the extra child benefit of £3.50 per week given to single parents (*Williams* (1981)).

(f) *Lump sums*

A lump sum order will generally be made in order to effect an equitable division of the parties' capital assets, or sometimes as a capitalisation of the wife's claims to periodical payments. A lump sum may be used in particular to compensate a wife for the loss of any pension expectations that may be a consequence of the divorce. There are problems connected with lump sums. Only one can be ordered (*Coleman* (1973)) and it cannot subsequently be varied (Matrimonial Causes Act, 1973, s.23 and 31). Consequently if a partner has expectations that have not yet been realised, for example under a will or an insurance policy, it is better for the application for a lump sum to be delayed or adjourned until the resources are available (*Hardy* (1981)).

(g) *Tax*

In general when assessing the resources available the court should base its calculation on the untaxed income of the spouses because the maintenance order itself will affect their tax liability. This rule was laid down in *Wachtel* (1973) and *Rodewald* (1977). The tax position of the parties on divorce is as follows. The ex-spouses will be assessed and taxed separately (see p.30) so that the ex-husband will not be entitled to the married mans' allowance. On the other hand he will be entitled to tax relief on any maintenance that he is ordered to pay by the court. The maintenance is regarded as a "charge" on his income. He will normally pay the maintenance, less tax, to his wife and account to the Inland Revenue for the tax deducted. If the wife is not liable to pay any tax, or all of the amount deducted, she can claim back any overpaid tax from the Inland Revenue. This is a bare explanation of a complex area of law that cannot be dealt with in full in this book but the following simplified example may help to illustrate how the system works:

Example:

H and W are divorced and H is ordered to pay to W £2,000 per year. She is looking after children whose maintenance is not included in this example but which entitles her to the additional personal tax allowance.

Husband's position	£	*Wife's position*	£
H's earnings	8,000	W's earnings	1,500
less: W's maintenance	2,000	*Gross* maintenance	2,000
	6,000	Total income	3,500
		less: personal and	
less: personal allowance	1,565	additional allowance	2,445
TAXABLE INCOME	4,435	TAXABLE INCOME	1,055
tax at 30%	1,330	tax at 30%	316

H's net income is therefore £6,670 from which he pays maintenance of £1,400 (£2,000 less tax @ 30%) and £600 tax on the maintenance to the Revenue.

But H has already paid tax on the maintenance of £600. This is £284 more than W's tax liability and she can reclaim this from the Revenue.

If the husband is also ordered to pay maintenance *direct* to a child not exceeding £1,565 per year (the amount of the personal allowance) then neither the child nor the wife would pay tax on that maintenance. Maintenance paid direct to a child is not regarded as part of the income of the mother. The husband would enjoy tax relief on the maintenance paid to a child in the same way as that paid to a wife and the child would recover the tax paid by him on the maintenance from the Revenue.

The wife in the above example has to go to the trouble of reclaiming tax from the Inland Revenue and can generally do so only if she produces a tax deduction certificate obtained from her husband. This can be tedious and husbands sometimes delay in sending the certificates. A simpler way of arranging these matters is available where the maintenance order qualifies as a "small maintenance payment" (Income and Corporation Taxes Act 1970, s.65). These are payments of up to £33 per week or £143 per month for a spouse, or £33 per week, £143 per month for payments made directly to a child. Where a payment is made to a person *for* a child the limits are £18 per week or £78 per month. Such payments are paid gross, *i.e.* without deduction of tax, by the husband. The payments are then treated as the taxable income of the wife (or child) and she pays tax on them if any tax is due.

(h) *Supplementary Benefit*

In general, the court will not take into account the fact that a wife may be entitled to supplementary benefit when assessing the amount of maintenance a husband should be required to pay. It is considered that the husband should not expect to be relieved of his liability to maintain his wife or children by the State. In any case he will be a liable relative under the Supplementary Benefit Act 1976 (see p.32) and can be required by the DHSS to make a contribution to his children's maintenance if they are in receipt of benefit. All the maintenance that a wife receives from her husband will be counted as her resources for supplementary benefit purposes and will reduce her entitlement accordingly. However a court will not generally make an order against a husband which reduces him to below subsistence level, which is interpreted to be what he would get from supplementary benefit were he entitled to it (*Shallow* (1978); *Fitzpatrick* (1979)). Therefore, at this level, the courts do take a wife's entitlement to benefit into account in that they recognise that where she is living at below subsistence level, she will be able to claim benefit. A husband reduced below this level by the obligation to pay maintenance will not generally be entitled to supplementary benefit, either because he is in full-time work or because maintenance is not deducted from his resources when assessing his right to benefit.

As explained on p.32 a husband is liable to maintain his children (but not a *divorced* wife) under the Supplementary Benefits Act 1976 and the DHSS is able to sue him for a contribution in the magistrates' courts if he does not pay voluntarily. The DHSS will be able to obtain such an order from the magistrates' court even though a final financial order has been made on divorce if it is considered that the order does not make an adequate contribution towards the maintenance of children. In *Hulley* v. *Thompson* (1981) a husband had transferred the home to his wife in full satisfaction of her claims to maintenance for herself and the children. It was nevertheless held that, when the wife claimed benefit, the DHSS could require the husband to make a contribution towards the maintenance of the children. However the financial order made on divorce would be taken into account in determining how much the husband had to pay.

A lump sum payment made on divorce will also be taken into account for supplementary benefit purposes. In general, where a person who claims benefit has *capital* resources of *under* £2,000 these are disregarded for benefit purposes. However, lump sums paid on divorce are an exception to this general rule. Lump sums of £2,000 or less which are paid by a liable relative (*i.e.* husband or ex-husband) are taken into account as *weekly income* calculated accordingly to a set formula the effect of which is to require the recipient to live on the lump sum at a level just above supplementary benefit level until the lump sum is exhausted. However it has been held that this rather stringent rule applies only to lump sums that are intended to replace an entitlement to periodic maintenance and not to a lump sum which represents a settlement of any property claims that a spouse may have against the other. Thus a lump sum paid to compensate a wife for her interest in the matrimonial home would not fall within this rule (Decision of the Social Security Commissioner, *R(SB)7/81*). Of course, where a claimant has capital in excess of £2,000 he is not entitled to benefit at all, wherever the capital came from.

3. Maintenance for children

Orders for financial provision for children do not depend on the successful outcome of their parents' divorce of other matrimonial proceedings. They can be made before a decree is granted, within a reasonable period of the dismissal of the suit, on granting a decree or at any time thereafter.

The only children in whose favour an order can be made are children of the family within the meaning of section 52(1) of the Matrimonial Causes Act 1973. The child must be the natural or adopted child of both of the parties, or any other child who has been treated by both of the parties as a child of the family, other than a child who has been boarded out with the parties by a local authority or voluntary organisation. A person can "treat" a child as one of his own family even if he is unaware of that child's true paternity (*W.* v. *W.* (1971)). A man will not be held to have treated as one of his family an unborn child, even where he marries the mother of that child in the mistaken belief that the child is his (*A*. v. *A*. (1974)). There must be a "family." Where an illegitimate child is born after the husband and wife have separated, it will not be a child of the husband's family even if the husband does agree to treat the child as his own (*Re M.* (1980)).

Initially provision cannot be made in favour of any child of over 18, and any order ceases to have effect once a child attains that age unless an application is made to extend the order where the child "is, or will be, or if such an order or provision were made would be, receiving instruction at an educational establishment or undergoing training for a trade, profession or vocation, whether or not he is also, or will be, in gainful employment." An order can also be extended beyond the age of 18 if there are special circumstances such as lack of earning capacity due to illness or other disability justifying an extended order. Normally any order for periodical payments is made to cease initially on the first birthday after passing the upper limit of compulsory school age, at present 16 (see s.29).

The matters which the court must consider in deciding what financial orders to make and the amount are "all the circumstances of the case", including in particular the following:

"(a) the financial needs of the child;
  (b) the income, earning capacity (if any), property and other financial resources of the child;
  (c) any physical or mental disability of the child;
  (d) the standard of living enjoyed by the family before the breakdown of the marriage;
  (e) the manner in which he was being and in which the parties to the marriage expected him to be educated or trained" (*ibid.* s.25(2)).

As with the maintenance of spouses on divorce or nullity, the court should seek, so far as it is practicable, to put the child in the financial position he or she would have enjoyed had the marriage not broken down and each parent had properly discharged his or her obligations.

Where financial provision in favour of a child of the family is sought from a party who is *not* the natural or adoptive parent of the child, the court in deciding whether and how to exercise its powers must in addition have regard to the following three considerations:

"(a) to whether that party had assumed any responsibility for the child's maintenance and, if so, to the extent to which, and the basis upon which, that party discharged such responsibility;

(b) to whether in assuming and discharging such responsibility that party did so knowing that the child was his or her own;

(c) to the liability of any other person to maintain the child" (*ibid.* s.25(3)).

Parties can make maintenance agreements in relation to children but they can never validly agree *not* to go to court for provision to be made. As already noted, it is generally advantageous from the tax point of view to have payments made directly to the child and not to the parent for the child. Whatever order is made, the parent is still entitled to give a good receipt for the payment and to come back to court to vary or enforce the order.

4. Property adjustment orders

The court has wide powers to transfer property from one spouse to the other or to the children. It may also make, vary or extinguish settlements under section 24 of the Matrimonial Causes Act 1973. These powers include a specific power to order a sale of property under the Matrimonial Homes and Property Act 1981 (no specific power of sale had been included in the 1973 Act, which caused some difficulties). The court rarely transfers property to children; indeed such transfers, which might have been used as a device for avoiding certain legal aid costs (the Law Society's charge on property recovered in legal proceedings), have been expressly disapproved of in *Drascovic* (1981).

The item of property most usually transferred from one spouse to the other under these powers is the matrimonial home. Sometimes a wife will accept such a transfer in place of periodical payments. Where there are minor children the spouse with custody will generally be allowed to occupy the home if this can be arranged until the children are of age. Orders known as *Mesher* orders were very popular at one time. A *Mesher* order is one under which both spouses retain a beneficial interest in the home, the wife and children are permitted to occupy it until the youngest child is of age and the home is then to be sold and the proceeds divided between the spouses. These orders are not now so popular. They cause difficulties in relation to liability for mortgage payments and for tax relief thereon, and the orders cannot be subsequently varied whatever injustice is caused at the time when the house has to be sold. In *Carson* (1981) a *Mesher* order has been made but the husband had fallen into arrears with the maintenance payments. The court had no power to compensate for this either by postponing the sale which had been ordered some years previously or by transferring to the wife the husband's interest in the home. One part of the problem in this case has now been remedied by the Matrimonial Homes and Property Act, s.8(2) as regards the date of sale, but it remains true that the rest of any *Mesher* order cannot be varied.

A more flexible way of dealing with the home, if it is not appropriate to transfer it outright to the spouse with custody, is to transfer it subject to a charge in favour of the non-custodial spouse, and give him a power to approach the court for an order for sale when that appears appropriate. The charge should be for a proportionate share in the proceeds of sale and not for a fixed sum so that it keeps pace with inflation and rises in house prices.

The court has power to transfer any "property" from one spouse to the other. This has been held to include a tenancy as well as owner occupied accommodation (*Thompson* (1976); *Regan* (1977)). However there is, in addition, a specific power to transfer secure tenancies covered by both the Rent Act and the Housing Act 1980 under the Matrimonial Homes Act 1967, s.7.

5. Variation of Orders

The court has power under section 31 to vary, discharge or suspend any order for periodical payments or other financial orders *except* an order for the payment of a lump sum or a property transfer order. An order for the sale of property can be varied (Matrimonial Homes and Property Act 1981, s.8(2)). Where a lump sum is ordered to be paid in installments the installments can be varied. If a wife's application for periodical payments has been dismissed with her consent then it appears that the order cannot be varied (*Dipper* (1980)).

In exercising its powers of variation the court must have regard to all the circumstances of the case, including any change in any of the matters to which the court was required to have regard when making the original order and, where the party against whom that order was made has died, the changed circumstances resulting from his or her death. Subject to these considerations, the court may make any order it thinks just in the changed circumstances, but is prohibited from ordering the payment of a lump sum or a property adjustment on an application to vary an order for periodical payments (*ibid.* s.31(5)).

An application for variation can be made at any time after the original order except that there is a time limit of six months from the grant of representation, which the court may extend, for an application by personal representatives of a deceased party who had been ordered to pay secured provision or by the person entitled to such payments (*ibid.* s.31(6)).

6. Avoidance of transaction intended to defeat claims for financial provision

Justice requires that no claim for financial relief or for its variation is defeated by the dishonest disposal of assets by the party liable to be ordered to provide it. Accordingly the court is by section 37 of the Act of 1973 empowered, whenever such a claim is pending, to restrain by injunction or other appropriate order any impending or threatened disposition of or dealing with the property or its transfer out of the jurisdiction if satisfied that it is intended to defeat a claim for financial provision, and to set aside certain past transactions entered into with a similar design. However, the court cannot set aside a disposition of property made for valuable consideration (*i.e.* a sale) to a person who acted in good faith and at the time of the disposition had no knowledge that the disposition was intended to defeat a spouse's claim for financial provision. Any disposition within the period of three years from the application for relief is presumed to have been made with this intent; any earlier dispositions must be proved by the applicant to have been made with such intent. An illustration of the operation of these provisions is provided by the case of *National Provincial Bank* v. *Hastings Car Mart* (1964), where a husband, intending to defeat his wife's claim to occupy the matrimonial home, sold it to a company which he controlled. The sale was set aside, the company having notice of the intent to defeat the wife's claim.

CHAPTER 9

RECOGNITION OF FOREIGN DECREES

A "limping marriage" is a marriage recognised as valid and subsisting in one country, and as dissolved and ended in another. The undesirability of such marriages is obvious. Their existence is due to a decree of divorce not necessarily receiving legal recognition outside the country which granted it.

In order to avoid the existence of these "limping marriages" a convention was concluded at the Hague in 1970 and signed by the United Kingdom. The Recognition of Divorces and Legal Separations Act was enacted in 1971 to bring the law in Great Britain into line with the convention and came into effect on January 1, 1972.

Under the Act any divorce or judicial separation obtained *by judicial or other proceedings* in a foreign country and recognised as effective in that country will be recognised as effective in Great Britain. One or both of the spouses must have been either habitually resident in that country or a national of it (1972 Act, s.3(1)). Any person who is domiciled in a country will be held to be habitually resident in it, but so may a person who is not domiciled in his country of residence (see p.14 on domicile). The courts in England will accept any finding of fact by a foreign court, including the fact of the parties' domicile, nationality or residence. This means that the English court will not have to be satisfied that a party was domiciled or habitually resident according to *English* law, but will accept the foreign court's adjudication on the matter (s.5(1)(2)). However, this recognition will only be extended to findings of fact by foreign courts where both parties took part in the proceedings.

One problem that has arisen in England because of the increasing number of Moslem immigrants in this country concerns the validity of the "talaq" form of divorce. This is a unilateral, non judicial form of divorce which will be recognised in England provided the talaq is pronounced in the country of which one or both of the spouses is a national or habitual resident. A pronouncement of a talaq divorce in England by, for example a national of Pakistan, will not be recognised as a valid divorce in England even though it would be so recognised in Pakistan (Domicile and Matrimonial Proceedings Act 1973, s.16 and *R.* v. *Registrar General, Ex p. Minhas* (1976)).

The validity of the talaq divorce has been considered by the House of Lords in *Quazi* (1980). By the law of Pakistan, where a husband sought a talaq divorce, notice had to be given to the wife and the divorce did not take effect until 90 days had elapsed, during which a reconciliation was attempted. It was held that a divorce by such procedure was valid, being a divorce by "other proceedings" under the Act. It is difficult to state what constitutes "proceedings" in this context. However proceedings which do not involve giving effective notice to the other spouse or which deny that spouse the opportunity to take part will not be recognised as creating a valid decree of divorce under section 8 of the Act (see below).

These new provisions replace the old law in England which had grown up through court decisions and had become rather complicated. There is one situation in which a foreign divorce has in the past been recognised by the English courts and which is preserved by the new Act. A divorce which has been obtained in a country other than that of the spouses' domicile and which is recognised as valid by the law of their country of domicile will also be recognised here (s.6(a)). Thus the case of *Armitage* v. *Att.-Gen.* (1906) would still be decided in the same way. In that case the spouses were domiciled in New York and the wife left the husband and got a divorce in South Dakota on a ground not recognised by the law of New York. However, the New York courts would have recognised the South Dakota decree as valid and therefore it was held that the English courts should also recognise its validity.

The recognition of foreign divorces is subject to a fundamental exception that such divorces will not be recognised if obtained by one spouse without the other being given reasonable notice of the proceedings or without being given a reasonable opportunity to take part in the proceedings.

In *Joyce* (1979) a wife who had been unable to get legal aid had done all she could to tell her husband's solicitors in Quebec that she wished to defend the divorce petition. The court was not told of this or of the fact that adultery and desertion had been found against the husband in magistrates' court proceedings in this country. The decree of the Quebec court was not recognised.

A decree will not be recognised if it would be manifestly contrary to public policy (s.8(2)). An example can be seen in the case of *Meyer* (1971) where a wife obtained a divorce from her Jewish husband in Germany in 1938. The husband had fled to England and she was told by her employer that she either divorced her husband or she lost her job and flat. She thought that she would be safer and better able to look after their daughter until they reached England if she got a divorce. After the husband's death the question arose as to whether she was his widow (and thus entitled to a widow's pension under the German Federal Compensation Law). It was held that the divorce would not be recognised as it was obtained by duress.

The Act is confined to the recognition of divorces and separations only. It does not require the English courts to recognise foreign maintenance, custody or other ancillary orders, nor the recognition of findings of fault made in divorce proceedings (s.8(3)). There are provisions, applicable to certain countries, for the reciprocal enforcement and recovery of maintenance under the Maintenance Orders (Reciprocal Enforcement) Act 1972. Most European countries are included in these provisions. The English courts have no power to make maintenance orders where they recognise a foreign divorce (*Turczak* (1970)).

PART III
CHILDREN

CHAPTER 10

PARENTAL RIGHTS, CUSTODY AND GUARDIANSHIP

1. Parental rights and duties

Both parents have equal parental rights and duties in relation to their legitimate children (Guardianship Act 1973, s.1). The mother alone has those rights and duties where the child is illegitimate. However it is often difficult to define or describe those parental rights and duties. An attempt to do so is contained in the Children Act 1975, s.85(1) which applies wherever the phrase "parental rights and duties" is used in that Act or in subsequent legislation. It is not, however, an enlightening definition. Parental rights and duties mean "all the rights and duties which by law the mother and father have in relation to a legitimate child and his property . . . and shall include a right of access and any other element included in a right or duty."

Whatever they are, it is clear that parental rights do not have the characteristics normally associated with rights. In particular they will rarely be enforced as such. A court will not give effect to a parental right if to do so would be contrary to the best interests of the child.

Another problem is isolating *parental* rights and duties from those rights and duties which may be imposed on or enjoyed by anyone who is caring for a child. A parent is said to have a duty to protect his child and to ensure that it is educated. But in fact anyone, parent or not, who cares for a child also has these duties.

The following are the main rights and duties associated generally, but not necessarily exclusively, with parenthood:–

(i)   the right to decide where and with whom the child shall live and associate,

(ii) the right to determine education, and the duty to educate,

(iii) the right to chastise reasonably,

(iv) the right and duty to protect and maintain the child,

(v) the right to manage the child's property (though, probably, not the right to make a claim to the services of the child),

(vi) the right to apply for a passport for the child,

(vii) the right to consent or refuse consent to medical treatment for the child (though the child himself may consent if over 16 and probably if below that age and capable of understanding the nature of his consent),

(viii) the right to give or refuse consent to adoption,

(ix) the right to give or refuse consent to the marriage of a child of between 16–18 years,

(x) the right to conduct or defend litigation on the child's behalf,

(xi) the right to succeed to the child's property on his death intestate.

As already noted the courts will not enforce these rights unless they are exercised in the interests of the welfare of the child. It is therefore possible *e.g.* to override parental refusal of consent to medical treatment (see *Re B* (1981) where parental refusal to consent to an operation on a baby suffering from Down's syndrome was overridden by the court in wardship proceedings), or a refusal to an adoption (see p.126).

The most important parental *duty* —to maintain the child—is enforced mainly in the context of matrimonial proceedings or custody proceedings under the Guardianship of Minors Act 1971, on which see page 95. The duty to care for and protect the child, which is imposed on anyone who is, for the time being, actually looking after a child and not just a parent, is enforced through the criminal law. Thus the Children and Young Persons Act 1933, s.1. makes it an offence to wilfully assault, ill-treat, neglect or abandon a child under 16. Other sections make it an offence to allow a child to reside in a brothel (s.3), cause him to go begging (s.4.) or give alcohol to a child under five (s.5). There are many other specific offences relating to children. The other main method whereby the courts can protect children from harm is via care proceedings (see p.137).

2. Custody

The right to the custody of a child is regarded as the most important parental right, from which all others flow. If a parent is deprived of custody by court order he then has few rights in relation to the child's upbringing except in so far as the court has specifically provided in the order, *e.g.* by providing for access. A parent deprived of custody can, of course, always apply again to the court for a variation of the order. It is also clear that succession rights (see above) are not terminated by a custody order. Nor is the right to consent or refuse consent to adoption. However all other rights—to determine education, home, religion, medical treatment, discipline etc.—are thought to be part and parcel of the right to custody. As Lord Justice Upjohn has said in *Re W.* (1964):

> "If an order is made granting custody of an infant to one parent without more, that would include care and control of that infant or, if the parent does not want care and control, power to direct with whom the infant shall reside; it also gives

that parent the right to organise the infant's religious and general education and his general upbringing. On the other hand, corresponding duties devolve on that parent. He has the duty of looking after and maintaining the child and giving proper thought to his religious and general education and upbringing generally."

In *Hewer* v. *Bryant* (1969) Sachs L.J. considered custody to be a "bundle of powers" ranging from physical control to administration of property. In *Dipper* (1980), however, it was denied that a parent having custody also had the right to decide education. This statement was *obiter* and is not thought to be correct.

Custody is equally divided between the mother and father of a legitimate child. On divorce the court can make joint custody orders and order that one parent has care and control. This is the preferred order where both parents are to play an active role in the lives of their children. If there is a dispute between the parents on the upbringing of the children then an application can be made to the court under the Guardianship Act 1973, s.1(3). However where parents have joint custody either parent can exercise any parental right by him or herself unless the other parent has signified his or her disapproval. There is no obligation to inform or consult the other parent (Guardianship Act 1973, s.1(1) and Children Act 1975, s.85(3)).

Any agreement under which a parent purports to give custody of his children to another is void. (Guardianship Act 1973, s.1(2); Children Act 1975, s.85(2)), but an agreement on custody made by a husband and wife on separation is valid but will be enforced by the court only if in the child's best interests. The mother and father of an illegitimate child cannot make a valid agreement that they shall have joint custody of their child. Nor is it possible for the court to make an enforceable joint custody order in favour of such parents whilst they continue to live together (Guardianship of Minors Act 1971, s.7). It follows that if the mother of an illegitimate child wishes the father to be able to exercise full parental rights this can be achieved only after her death; the mother may appoint him guardian in her will. It is not possible to confer full parental rights on him whilst they are living together.

(a) *Principles upon which custody and access will be decided*

"Where in any proceeding before any court . . . the custody or upbringing of a minor . . . is in question, the court, in deciding that question, shall regard the welfare of the minor as the first and paramount consideration, and shall not take into consideration whether from any other point of view the claim of the father, or any right at common law possessed by the father, in respect of such custody or upbringing . . . is superior to that of the mother or the claim of the mother is superior to that of the father" (Guardianship of Minors Act 1971, s.1).

In *J*. v. *C*. (1970) the House of Lords decided that this provision applies not only to disputes concerning a child between parents, but between parents and strangers and between strangers and strangers. This famous case, in which the upbringing of a boy aged 10 was entrusted to English foster-parents in preference to his natural Spanish parents of unblemished character, further lays down that "the rights and wishes of parents, whether unimpeachable or otherwise, must be assessed and weighted in their bearing on the welfare of the child in conjunction with all other relevant factors . . . and that there is no rule of law that the rights and wishes of unimpeachable parents must prevail over other considerations although such rights and wishes, recognised as they are by nature and society, can be capable of ministering to the total welfare of the child in a special way, and must therefore preponderate in many cases."

The court is not, therefore concerned either to reward or punish parents in awarding custody, nor is it concerned with giving effect to parental "rights" (*S*. v. *S*. (1976)). In *D*. v. *D*. (1967) the mother, who had committed adultery, "kidnapped" the children whilst they were out walking. It was nevertheless decided that the best interests of the children required that she be given their custody, although nothing was said against the father.

The factor to which courts give most weight is the need to maintain stability for the child. In the vast majority of cases the court will be unwilling to move a child from a home and environment in which it is settled. The normal custody order therefore preserves the *status quo* unless serious allegations of incompetence or an undesirable mode of life are made against the person with actual custody. In addition to this factor the courts will consider others though, as was said in *Re F*. (1969), these cases cannot be dealt with by totting up points for or against a parent. The factors that will be considered are:

(a) the wishes of the child, if old enough to express them, but such wishes may be disregarded.
(b) the age of the child—a baby or very young child is sometimes thought to be better looked after by its mother.
(c) the undesirability of separating brothers and sisters.
(d) the religious beliefs of the parents. A court will not wish to unsettle established beliefs, neither will it wish a child to be

brought up in an isolated way, deprived of contact with persons other than the adherants of a particular small religious sect. (see *Re H*. (1980)).
(e) the stability of the home and, in particular, the character of any step-parent and his or her willingness to accept the child.
(f) the "character" of a parent. An "unconventional" parent, *e.g.* a homosexual or one adopting an unusual life style, will find it more difficult to obtain custody than a "conformist" parent.

Decisions are always determined by the infinite variety of circumstances to be found in the individual cases and therefore reported decisions are a fallible guide to the outcome of future cases. There is now greater willingness in the appellate courts to change the lower courts' decision not only on the ground that the wrong legal principles were applied, but also on the ground that the decision was unjust or wrong in fact (*Re F*. (1976)). It must also be remembered that an order for custody is not final as either parent may apply to the court for the variation or revocation of the existing order.

Custody may be granted to a third party, *e.g.* a grandparent, in both matrimonial and guardianship proceedings. However a third party is not able to *initiate* custody proceedings, this can be done only by the parents or by one of a married couple instituting matrimonial proceedings. A third party who is concerned about the upbringing of a child may, however, get the child made a ward of court and ask for care and control (see p.120). The court may also put the child into the care of a local authority if it considers that there are "exceptional circumstances" making this desirable (Matrimonial Causes Act 1973, s.43(1)); Domestic Proceedings and Magistrates' Courts Act 1978, s.10(*a*); Guardianship Act 1973, s.2(2)).

(b) *Access*

A parent deprived of custody, or care and control, is normally entitled to "reasonable access" unless the court makes an order forbidding it. Such an order is made only in very exceptional circumstances when it has clearly been proved that any degree of access under any conditions (which a court in its discretion is empowered to impose) is likely to be seriously detrimental to a child (*B*. v. *B*. (1971). In *Rashid* (1979) a father who had taken the children to Pakistan in breach of a court order which seriously affected the children's health was refused access. In a recent case, *M*. v. *M*. (1973), the court suggested that access was really a right of the *child* to see its own parent rather than a parental right. If parents

can agree between themselves the duration, frequency and circumstances of access, a court does not generally interfere. But if they
cannot agree, or their agreement does not sufficiently take into
account the needs or wishes of a child, there is power for making an
order which, if necessary, lays down in complete detail all matters
relating to access. In granting access to a parent living in adultery
the court may prohibit contact between the child and the other party
to the adultery. This condition may be imposed also where the
parent has a homosexual relationship.

(c) *Arrangements*

In proceedings for divorce, nullity or judicial separation, whether
defended or undefended, the court is, regardless of the requirements
or wishes of the parties, concerned with the welfare of any child of
the family up to the age of 16 or beyond if his education continues.
"Child of the family" is defined in section 52 of the Matrimonial
Causes Act 1973 as including any child "treated" by both of the
spouses as a child of their family. In deciding whether a child has
been so treated, lack of knowledge on the part of one or both parties
as to the child's paternity is immaterial. (*W. (R.J.)* v. *W. (S.J.)*
(1972). As we have seen, there is a prohibition against the making of
a decree absolute of divorce or nullity or of a decree of judicial
separation until, generally speaking, the court is satisfied with
regard to the arrangements of all such children (Matrimonial
Causes Act 1973, s.41), and failure to abide by this requirement will
render the decree void.

(d) *Practice and procedure*

Divorce courts

The court has jurisdiction to make orders over all children of the
family under 18 (Matrimonial Causes Act 1973, s.52). As already
indicated it can make a joint custody order and give actual care and
control to one parent. This should be done only where the parents
are capable of cooperating (*Jussa* (1972)). Alternatively both custody
and care can be vested in one spouse, or custody given to one, care to
the other. Custody may be granted to a third party, *e.g.* a
grandmother or other relative. Finally in "exceptional circumstances" a supervision order or care order may be made in favour of
the local authority. (1973 Act, ss.43, 44).

The powers of the court relating to children may be invoked at
any time in the course of proceedings, and orders may be made not
only before, on or after the final decree but also, where the
proceedings are dismissed, at the time of the dismissal, or within a

reasonable period afterwards (1973 Act, s.42(1)). Although there is jurisdiction to make orders for custody in respect of children over the age of 16 such orders are not generally made beyond this age.

In exercising their jurisdiction over children the divorce courts have available for their assistance specially appointed probation officers who are for this purpose known as court welfare officers. Their functions and the procedure applicable to their reports, are laid down by the Matrimonial Causes Rules. Contested matters relating to children are not heard in open court but "in chambers"—a private and essentially informal hearing in a judge's private room or other convenient accommodation to which neither the press nor public are admitted. (For the court's power regarding maintenance of children, see p.95).

Magistrates' courts

The jurisdiction of the magistrates' courts over children in matrimonial proceedings is now governed by the Domestic Proceedings and Magistrates' Courts Act 1978. This Act also amends their powers under the Guardianship of Minors Act 1971 so as to bring them into line with their powers in matrimonial proceedings and also make them similar to the powers exercised by the divorce courts. For example the definition of "child of the family" (see p.95) is now the same in both courts. Jurisdiction in both courts extends to children up to the age of 18.

The courts' powers are wide and may be exercised irrespective of the wishes of the parents and regardless of whether the complaint succeeds or is dismissed (1978 Act, s.8). Magistrates also have powers to give custody to a third party or to commit the child to the care of the local authority in "exceptional circumstancs."

Under the 1978 Act magistrates do not have the power to make joint custody orders. Legal and actual custody can be granted to only one person. However they can make an order which has virtually the same effect as one for joint custody. The court may direct that the parent deprived of actual custody shall exercise such other custodial functions as the court may specify jointly with the custodial parent (1978 Act, s.8(4)). It might have been simpler to confer a jurisdiction to make joint custody orders.

In making a custody or access order the Magistrates can call for a welfare report at any stage in the proceedings. The report will normally be written by a local authority social worker. A copy should be given to the parties "either before or during the hearing" (1978 Act, s.12).

For maintenance orders relating to children see p.56.

3. Guardianship

A guardian is a person who acquires most parental rights, powers and duties on the death of one or both of the parents. Either parent may, by deed or will, appoint a guardian with effect from his or her death (Guardianship of Minors Act 1971, s.4). Such a guardian will become a joint guardian with the surviving parent. If there is any conflict between guardian and parent then the guardian can apply to the court under section 4 of the Guardianship of Minors Act 1971. The court then may refuse to make any order (which has the effect of leaving the surviving parent the sole guardian of the child) or order that the guardian act as sole guardian, or jointly with the surviving parent. It may further make such orders as to custody and access as it thinks fit in the interests of the child. The court can also order the mother or father to pay reasonable maintenance for the child to the guardian (1971 Act, s.10).

A court has power to appoint a guardian if a deceased parent has not appointed a guardian or the appointed guardian or guardians are dead or refuse to accept office or the child in question has no parent or guardian or any person having parental rights with respect to him (ss.3 and 5). In any of these circumstances anybody interested in the welfare of the child may apply to the court, which may appoint whom it likes although it tends to give preference to blood relations and does not generally appoint strangers when fit persons are to be found amongst the relations.

A guardian who has accepted office cannot resign without leave of the High Court. On the other hand he can be removed by order of this court if the welfare of a child requires it (1971 Act, s.6). Guardianship terminates automatically on a child attaining his majority or his earlier marriage or death.

4. Custodianship

A new power to apply to the court for the custody of a child was introduced by the Children Act 1975 which the Act calls a "custodianship order," thus adding yet another method by which the custody of a child may be claimed. These provisions are not yet in force and no date has been set at the time of writing for their commencement. There appears to be some doubt as to whether they will ever come into force now.

The problem that these new provisions were designed to solve is that under existing legislation it is difficult for a person who is not a parent of a child to initiate custody proceedings. For example, take the case of a grandmother who is looking after her grandchild and fears that the child's father wishes to take the child from her. If she wants to get a custody order she will find that she cannot use the

Guardianship of Minors Act 1971 as she is not the child's parent, nor, obviously, will she be able to avail herself of the matrimonial legislation to get a custody order, nor can she be appointed a guardian as the child's father is still alive. At present the only solution is to have the child made a ward of court (see p.120) which is not only expensive but is also an inappropriate method of solving a simple dispute about custody. Step-parents and foster-parents are in a similar position. Accordingly, under the Children Act 1975, s.33(3), the following persons are enabled to apply for a custodianship order:

(a) a relative or step-parent with whom the child has lived for three months who applies with the consent of the person having legal custody of the child (provided the child has not been named in matrimonial proceedings as a "child of the family"),

(b) any person with whom the child has lived for periods amounting to 12 months (including the last three months) with the consent of the person having legal custody (*e.g.* a foster-parent provided the natural parent consents),

(c) any person with whom the child has lived for periods amounting to three years (including the last three months). No consent is needed here and this provision is intended to assist the long term foster-parent.

Access for the child's parents can be ordered under section 34 and an order can be made requiring them to contribute towards the child's maintenance. A most important provision is contained in section 41 which makes it an offence to remove a child from its home without leave of the court where a custodianship order has been applied for by a person qualified under heading (c) above. A parent cannot therefore in such a case exercise his "right" to custody and remove the child (if he could then the application for custodianship would fail as the child would not have had his home with the applicant for the three months immediately prior to the application).

Chapter 11

ILLEGITIMACY AND LEGITIMATION

Many of the old distinctions between the legitimate and the illegitimate child have now been abolished or eroded and the social stigma of being illegitimate has greatly diminished. Nevertheless the concept still exists in English law and there are still important legal differences between the legitimate and the illegitimate child, especially in relation to maintenance and legal position of the father of the child. The Law Commission has produced a working paper (No. 74, 1979) which puts forward the case for abolishing the separate status of illegitimate. A final report, which is not expected to be quite so radical, is expected in 1982.

1. Illegitimacy and legitimation

Whether a child is legitimate or illegitimate is determined by the rules of common law as modified by modern statutes, which in certain circumstances confer the status of legitimacy on some children who would otherwise be illegitimate.

At common law a child is legitimate only if his parents were lawfully married either at the time of his conception, even if the marriage had ended by death or divorce before his birth, or at the time of the child's birth although he was conceived before his parents were married.

The first statutory modification was made by the Legitimacy Act 1926, which introduced the principle of legitimation into English law. Its effect is to render legitimate a living illegitimate child whose parents marry at any time after his birth. Since the enactment of the Legitimacy Act 1959 (now the Legitimacy Act 1976, s.2) legitimation operates even though one or both of the parents were married to a third person at the time of the child's birth, but it applies only if the father was domiciled in England at the time of the marriage. The parents of legitimated children are under a duty to re-register his birth and are liable to be fined if they fail to do so. The legal rights and duties of a legitimated person are, generally speaking, the same as those of a person born legitimate.

The other statutory modifications relate to children of voidable and of void marriages (see p.79). As a decree of nullity in a voidable marriage no longer has any retrospective effect, it is clear that any children of a voidable marriage are legitimate (Matrimonial Causes Act 1973, s.16) and a child of a void marriage is equally treated as legitimate provided that at the time when its conception must have taken place, or (if later) at the time of the celebration of the marriage, either parent, or both, reasonably believed that their marriage was valid (Legitimacy Act 1976, s.1; *Hawkins* v. *Att-Gen* (1966)). The father of the child must have been domiciled in England at the time of the child's birth or, if he died before this event, at the time of his death.

2. Proof of paternity

Proof of paternity was almost impossible in the past and is still difficult despite the availability of blood tests. Accordingly the law relied, and still relies, heavily on presumption. A child born to a married woman is presumed to be legitimate, that is the father of the child is presumed to be the mother's husband. The burden of proving that such a child is illegitimate is therefore placed on the person alleging it. The burden of proof used to be heavy—proof beyond all reasonable doubt as in criminal cases. This has now been changed by the Family Law Reform Act 1969, s.26 which provides that :

> "Any presumption of law as to the legitimacy or illegitimacy of any person may in any civil proceedings be rebutted by evidence which shows that it is more probable than not that the person is illegitimate or legitimate, as the case may be, and it shall not be necessary to prove that fact beyond reasonable doubt in order to rebut the presumption."

Evidence of paternity may consist of proof that a couple were cohabiting at the time of conception or that the alleged father had assumed responsibility for the child or acknowledged the child as his. Where a woman was having intercourse with more than one man at the time of conception often it will be impossible to say which was the father in the absence of blood test evidence.

Blood tests can show that a certain man *cannot* be the father of a particular child where the child's blood has characteristics that were not inherited from the mother and could not have been inherited from the man alleged to be the father. The tests therefore produce negative not positive results though where either father or child have rare blood characteristics the test may show that it is highly likely that a particular man is the father.

The use of blood tests in all civil matters, including matrimonial affiliation proceedings, is now governed by Part III of the Family Law Reform Act 1969. It enables any court in which the paternity of a person falls to be determined, on application by a party to the proceedings, to "give a direction for the use of blood tests to ascertain whether such tests show that a party to the proceedings is or is not thereby excluded from being the father of that person and for the taking, for the purpose of these tests, of blood samples from that person, the mother of that person and any party alleged to be the father of that person."

A blood sample may be taken only with a person's consent subject to two exceptions. The first one concerns a child under the age of 16. Such a child is incapable of giving his consent, but the person who has the care and control of him may consent for him. Children involved in litigation are often represented by the Official Solicitor, as guardian *ad litem*, who will only consent to a blood test on the child if he thinks it in the child's best interests. If he refuses consent, the court may order a test and will in general do so where the interests of justice make it necessary and where it is not clearly contrary to the interests of the child (*S.* v. *S.* (1970)). On balance the court will lean in favour of giving consent to making a blood test on a child as it is considered better for all that all the relevant evidence is revealed. However it will not so order if the question of paternity is not central to the litigation. In *Re J.S.* (1980) the child was clearly illegitimate and either A or B could be the father. The mother lived with A and B made the child a ward of court and sought to establish paternity in order to get access. It was held that as he would not get access in any event it was not in the child's best interest to raise the issue of paternity.

Secondly, where a person is suffering from a mental disorder and cannot validly consent the person who has care and control may consent to a blood test on his behalf. The patient's doctor must certify that the taking of the sample will not prejudice his care and treatment.

Apart from these two exceptions a blood test may be taken only with consent. If a court orders a test and a person refuses to consent the test cannot be made but "the court may draw such inferences, if any, from the facts as appear proper in the circumstances" In particular if the person claiming relief seeks to rely on the presumption of legitimacy, such as a married woman seeking maintenance from her husband for her child, then, if she refuses to consent to a blood test, the court may dismiss her claim even where there is no other evidence to rebut the presumption.

The question of paternity generally arises in the context of matrimonial, guardianship, or affiliation proceedings, or sometimes in relation to disputes over wills. There is no procedure whereby a person can apply for a declaration of paternity alone (though the Law Commission is likely to recommend that this be introduced). There is a procedure whereby a person can apply for a declaration of *legitimacy* without applying for any other relief (Matrimonial Causes

Act 1973, s.45). A person who fails to establish that he or she is the legitimate child of his parents cannot however go on and get the court to declare who is his father. A petition of this nature can be brought only if the petitioner is a British subject or his right to be treated as a British subject depends at least in part on his legitimacy or the validity of any marriage, and either he is domiciled in England or Northern Ireland or he claims any real or personal estate in England. A petition for declaration of legitimacy must be brought in the High Court, but a petition for a declaration of legitimation may be brought in the High Court or a county court. The Attorney-General must be made a party, and any declaration resulting from a petition binds all persons who have given notice unless it is subsequently proved to have been obtained by fraud or collusion.

3. Affiliation

The only way in which a woman can obtain a maintenance order from the father in respect of their illegitimate child is to issue affiliation proceedings in the magistrates' courts under the Affiliation Proceedings Act 1957. She can apply for maintenance for her child only, not for herself. The child has no independent right to apply for maintenance.

The mother must issue a summons against the man alleged to be the father. If she is successful he is adjudged the "putative father" and may be ordered to pay the following:

(a) weekly maintenance to the child, or to herself for the child,
(b) a lump sum of up to £500, which in particular may be ordered to meet expenses already incurred in connection with the needs of the child, including any funeral expenses (Domestic Proceedings and Magistrates Courts Act 1978 s.50(2)).

There is no power to order settlements or transfers of property in favour of illegitimate children.

The mother must be a "single woman" at the time of her application or at the child's birth. For this purpose a woman is "single" not only if she is unmarried, widowed or divorced, but also if she is married but has lost her *common law* right to be maintained by her husband (see p.17; *Gaines* v. *W.* (1968)). She must be living apart from her husband. All parties must be resident in England and Wales but the nationality or domicile of any of them is irrelevant (*R.* v. *Bow Road Domestic Proceedings Court, ex p. Adegiba* (1968)).

It was only with great reluctance, and with the aim of relieving the Poor Law authorities of some expenses, that the power to apply for a maintenance order against a putative father was first enacted in 1834. The Act made the unusual requirement that the mother's evidence had to be corroborated in a material particular, such mothers being then regarded as "shameless and unprincipled" in the words of the Poor Law Commissioners. This requirement has persisted through a number of legislative changes and still remains, though much criticised. A defendant can, therefore, be adjudged a putative father only if the mother's own testimony is "corroborated in some material particular" by evidence other than her own, for example, that the applicant and the defendant were going out together or had been seen kissing or behaving affectionately. However the Affiliation Proceedings (Amendment) Act 1972 does provide some help to the mother of an illegitimate child. Where the putative father does not defend the action, she need not give evidence in person (s.1). Also the previous time limit within which a mother must bring an action has been extended from one to three years. There is no time limit if the defendant paid money for the child's maintenance during its first year. If the defendant left England before the child's birth, the summons must be issued within three years of his return.

An order is now payable for the same length of time as is the case of legitimate children, that is they are payable initially up to the age of 18 and may continue after than (with no age limit) if the child is still receiving education or training or where there are special circumstances (Domestic Proceedings and Magistrates Courts Act 1978, s.52). The order is payable either to the mother for the child, or direct to the child, which can provide a considerable benefit to the mother in relation to her liability for tax (see further p.93). An illegitimate person over 18 can himself apply for an extension of the order beyond the age of 18 (but he cannot apply for an order *de novo*) and the payments will then be made to him personally (Family Law Reform Act 1969, s.5(2)).

On what basis are orders made? The 1978 Domestic Proceedings and Magistrates' Courts Act requires the same considerations to be taken into account as where maintenance for a child is ordered in matrimonial proceedings in the Magistrates' Courts (s.50(2)). Thus, income, earning capacity, responsibilities, needs, etc., are all taken into account. The father's financial position will be taken into account—maintenance is not confined to "necessities" or determined by the mother's standard of living (*Haroutunian* v. *Jennings* (1977)).

Custody or access is not determined under the Affiliation Proceedings Act 1957. A father wishing to claim custody or access must apply under the Guardianship of Minors Act 1971, s.9 to the

High, County or Magistrates' Courts. Of course if he has never looked after the child he is unlikely to get custody but the courts now consider that it is normally appropriate to grant access (*M.* v. *J.* (1978)). The fact that the child is illegitimate should not affect the issue—it is purely a question of what is in the child's best interests.

The consent of a father to the adoption of his illegitimate child is required only if he has been granted custody of the child by the court (Children Act 1975, s.107(1)). The putative father who is paying maintenance for the child is, however, entitled to know of and be heard at the adoption hearing. It is normal practice in many cases for the child's guardian *ad litem* in adoption proceedings to seek out the putative father and ask if he has any views on the adoption. As a last resort the father could attempt to prevent adoption by making an application for custody (*Re C. (M.A.)* (1966)). This and the adoption application would then be heard together.

CHAPTER 12

WARDSHIP

Wardship jurisdiction, which is exclusive to the Family Division of the High Court, is an historical survival from feudal times. Through the centuries it has continually changed is character in response to changing social conditions. A typical modern ward of court is no longer an orphan whose property needs protection, but a young child of a broken home or a child in care. In 1980 1,962 applications were made to make children wards of court. Wardship, therefore concerns a relatively small number of children and families, but it performs a useful function for them partly because of its special powers and partly because it is the only legal remedy in some situations. A child cannot be made a ward after reaching the age of 18 (Family Law Reform Act 1969, s.1; Sched. 3, para. 3(1)).

Wardship proceedings are commenced by the issue of an originating summons. The immediate and automatic effect of a summons is to make the child in question a ward for 21 days from the date of issue. After the expiration of this period the child ceases to be a ward unless application has been made meanwhile for the hearing of the summons. If an application is made the child continues to be a ward until the date of the hearing which, if the proceedings are contested, may be a long time ahead, and the future beyond that date depends on the judge's decision. A judge can at any time from the very beginning of the proceedings order that a child shall be "dewarded." Marriage does not terminate wardship but a ward ceases to be a ward on reaching his majority on his eighteenth birthday.

Wardship proceedings are heard in private. The evidence is given by sworn written statements or orally or by a mixture of both methods. In most cases the judge has the benefit of a full report prepared by experienced staff in the office of the Official Solicitor after a thorough investigation of the case, including interviews with all parties concerned and, if appropriate, consultation with specialists. The Official Solicitor in performing these functions is not for or against anybody. His sole concern is to give every possible assistance to the judge in the interests of the child's welfare. The contents of his report are not necessarily made available to the parties as the judge may in his discretion withhold it from them (*Re K.* (1965)).

A ward's custody vests in the court and his daily "care and control" in whomsoever the court appoints, subject to the court's directions and approval of all major decisions. The powers of wardship jurisdiction are virtually unlimited and now include the power to commit to the care of a local authority and the making of a supervision order (Family Law Reform Act 1969, s.7). The powers also include the making of orders relating to care and control, maintenance, access, religious upbringing, education, restrictions on leaving the jurisdiction, prohibition of undesirable associations of marriage and the administration or protection of the ward's property. The court may, therefore, not merely determine to whom "care and control" should be committed and how the ward is to be brought up, but it can make orders binding on the ward, for example, where he is to live, and restraining third parties from associating, communicating or marrying the ward. Interference with a ward involving disobedience of an order of the court constitutes "contempt of court" and is punishable by imprisonment or fining of the offender. The ward himself is similarly liable to punishment if he flouts orders binding on him.

In proceedings for divorce, nullity or judicial separation a judge may at any time direct that a wardship summons should issue so that any child who requires it is given this method of protection (Matrimonial Causes Act 1973, s.42). Subject to this power, which is rarely exercised, a child may be made a ward of court only on the application by either parent, including the father of an illegitimate child, or by another "interested person" for example, a grandparent or foster parent (Practice Direction (1967)). Wardship proceedings are nowadays used increasingly by local authorities in cases where the child protection legislation is inappropriate or, in the local authorities' view, does not confer upon them sufficient powers.

The following are typical situations in which wardship jurisdiction is invoked by parents or interested third parties :

(a) When the dispute concerns a child between the ages of 16 and 18 the jurisdiction is virtually exclusive as magistrates' courts have no power to make an order in respect of this age group unless a child is physically or mentally incapable of self-support, and the divorce courts as a rule of practice make an order affecting a child over the age of 16, other than an order for maintenance or education, only in exceptional circumstances.

(b) Where any of the special remedies available in wardship proceedings are required for the protection of the child. An example is *Re X* (1975) in which a girl's step-father made her a ward of court and asked that the publication of a book containing details of the sordid life of her dead father be prevented in order to protect the ward from harm. The order was refused but the court had no doubt that it could make such an order in an appropriate case.

(c) Where an immediate embargo is required on a child leaving or being removed from the country.

(d) Where a third party with an interest in the child considers that the guidance and protection of the court is required. An example is *Re D.* (1976) where a mother consented to the sterilisation of her 11 year old mentally handicapped daughter. An educational psychologist made the girl a ward of court and the court ordered that the operation should not take place, (see also *Re B.* (1981), where the court was asked for its consent to an operation on a baby born with Down's syndrome).

(e) Where any of the parties concerned wish to protect the welfare and future of a child after a mother's withdrawal of consent to its proposed adoption or the natural father of an illegitimate child has intervened to prevent its adoption (*Re E.* (1964).

(f) Where a local authority considers its powers under the child protection legislation are inadequate, *e.g.* where a parent of a child in care under section 2 of the Child Care Act 1980 wishes to take the child back against the wishes of the local authority.

It is in connection with the use by local authorities of the wardship jurisdiction that most problems have arisen recently. There is no doubt that the court will use this jurisdiction in order to supplement the powers of the local authority (*Re D.* (1977); *A.* v. *Liverpool City Council* (1981)). It can also be invoked by a parent or other interested person if the local authority has acted in breach of its statutory powers (*Re L.* (A.C.) (1971)). Moreover once the child in care *is* a ward of court, whoever applied, the local authority cannot make any decisions in relation to the child, or move him from his home, without asking the consent of the court. (*Re Clare* (1980)). However, it has now been established by the House of Lords that the court will not interfere with a local authority's discretion in deciding how a child in care should be looked after. This is a matter for the local authority. In *A.* v. *Liverpool City Council* (1981) the mother of a child in care was suddenly deprived of access to the child by the local authority. She applied to have the child made a ward of court and for access to be ordered in her favour. The House of Lords refused, considering that the question of access was a matter that Parliament had entrusted the local authority to decide under the Child Care Act 1980 and related legislation.

Jurisdiction

Wardship jurisdiction extends to children who are British subjects regardless of their whereabouts at the time of proceedings. Otherwise it extends to children of any nationality or domicile provided they are physically within the jurisdiction when the summons is issued.

While physical presence confers jurisdiction, the court is very reluctant to make a foreign child a ward of court if he has been kidnapped into the jurisdiction, particularly where a foreign court has already made an order in respect of the child (*Re E.* (1967)).

Re T. (1968) was a case of this kind. It concerned two young children, aged six and five respectively, who were born to an Englishwoman who married a Canadian in Alberta in 1961 and lived with him there until 1967. In that year, while the father was on holiday, the mother took the children to England without his knowledge or consent. After her arrival she made them wards of court by issuing a wardship summons in order to enable her to resist a demand for their return by her husband, an artisan with a good job in Canada, who had followed in order to get the children back. In her evidence in support of her claim for the children the mother made complaints about her husband's matrimonial conduct towards her but there was no evidence before the court to suggest that her husband was not a reasonable father or that the children might come to harm if returned to Canada. In ordering the children's return to their father and making an order that they should cease to be wards on leaving England it was said in the Court of Appeal:

> "This Court sets itself against these unilateral movements of children, which have been far too frequent in the last few years . . . It seems . . . that the removal of children from their home and their surroundings by one of their parents who happens to live in or have connections with another country is a thing against which the court should set its face, and that, unless there is good reason to the contrary, it should not countenance proceedings of that kind."

Recent cases, however, have emphasised that in these, as in other cases, the welfare of the child is of paramount consideration and an order should not be made to penalise a 'kidnapping" parent (*Re L.* (1974)). Moreover no order sending a child out of the country should be made on an *ex parte* application, only when the full facts can be considered (*Re C.* (1976)).

CHAPTER 13

ADOPTION

Adoption was unknown to English law until 1926 when the first Adoption Act was passed by Parliament. Adoption gradually increased in popularity as is shown by the annual growth of orders up to 1968 when 26,986 orders were made in Great Britain. There has since been a decline and in 1979 only 10,870 orders were made. This is probably due to the fact that fewer babies are now offered for adoption. However it is also clear that many adoptions nowadays are not cases of babies being adopted by "strangers," but are made in favour of parents and step-parents in respect of children they are already looking after.

1. Legislation on adoption

The legislation covering adoption is in an incredibly confusing state. There are Adoption Acts of 1958, 1960, 1964 and 1968. These enactments have been extensively changed by the Children Act 1975. Some, but not all, of the provisions of the Children Act 1975 came into force in November 1976 and some subsequently. It appears that the provisions of the Act relating to adoption will not come into force fully until the end of 1982 or even later. To add to the confusion, an Adoption Act was passed in 1976 which consolidated all the previous legislation on adoption. However it is not in force, and will not be brought into force until the Children Act 1975 is fully in operation.

In an attempt to minimise this confusion the first references in the following pages are to the Children Act 1975 or other existing enactments. References to the Adoption Act 1976 follow in square brackets. It is indicated in the text which of the provisions of the Children Act are not yet in force.

2. What is adoption?

The legal effect of an adoption order is to obliterate the existing legal relationship between natural parents and their child, whether it is legitimate or illegitimate, and to create a new legal relationship of parent and child between adopter or adopters and the adopted child. An adoption order, accordingly, permanently deprives natural parents of any rights or duties whatever in respect of their child and vests in them instead in the adopters. There is only one situation where an adoption order can be revoked, and that is where an adopted child is legitimated by the marriage of its parents (Adoption Act 1960, s.1(1) [Adoption Act 1976, s.52]).

As already mentioned although many adoptions are of babies by married couples who are unable to have children of their own, an increasing number of adoptions are made in favour of adopters who are related to the child. Examples are:

(a) the adoption of an illegitimate child by its own mother on her own (*Re D.* (An Infant) (1959));

(b) the adoption of an illegitimate child by its own mother and her husband (the child's stepfather);

(c) the adoption of a legitimate child of a former marriage by its mother and her second husband (the child's stepfather);

(d) the adoption of a child by grandparents (*Re D.X.* (1949)) or by a married brother or sister of the parent and their respective spouses.

The Children Act 1975, s.11 leans heavily against adoption by one parent alone as in (a) above unless the other parent is lost, dead or there is some other reason which justifies his exclusion. It is considered that it will generally be in a child's best interests to retain contact with his natural father [Adoption Act 1976, s.15(3)]. Similarly the Act leans against adoption by a step-parent and parent as in (c) above if it is considered that the matter would be better dealt with by making a custody or joint custody order under the Matrimonial Causes Act 1973, s.42. The court should also consider whether or not the matter would be better dealt with by a custodianship order (see *ante* p.112) rather than by adoption. This latter provision has not yet been implemented and no plans to implement it exist at the time of writing. (Children Act 1975, s.37(1).)

3. Who may adopt and be adopted

Any person who is under 18, who has never been married and who lives in England and Wales may be adopted.

A couple may adopt a child only if they are married and both aged 21 or over. Single persons over 21 may also adopt a child. Under the Children Act 1975, s.11 a single parent adopting his child must also be 21. Under the old law a parent could adopt although under 21 [Adoption Act 1976 s.15].

The child must have lived with the prospective adopters continuously for at least three months, disregarding the first six weeks of life. This is to give both adopters and the local authority or other agency time to find out whether or not the child and adopters are suited. During this period the child becomes a "protected child" under the 1958 Adoption Act s.37(1)(*b*) (see *post* p.130).

One of the aims of the Children Act 1975 was to discourage private placements for adoption, that is placements other than by registered agencies. Non-agency adoptions cannot be banned altogether because many adoptions are by relatives or long term foster parents in which no agency is involved, but which could not be banned or discouraged. The solution adopted is the introduction of different "probationary" periods. If the adopters are parents, step parents or relatives or if the adoption has been arranged by an agency, then the adopters must have cared for the child at least 13 weeks (and the child must be at least 19 weeks old). In all other cases, *e.g.* where no adoption agency has been involved and the adoptive parents are "strangers" to the child, then the child must have lived continuously with the adopters for 12 months before the order can be made. (Children Act 1975, s.9 [Adoption Act 1976, s.13].). These provisions came into force in February 1982.

4. Consents

An adoption order cannot be made unless both parents and any guardian of a legitimate child, or the mother or guardian of an illegitimate child, have given their consent, or a court has made an order dispensing with any necessary consent. (For the position of the father of an illegitimate child, see p.119).

For a consent to be valid it must be in writing and, if executed in the United Kingdom, attested by a justice of the peace, justices' clerk or county court officer in order to ensure its authenticity and that it is given voluntarily. A mother's consent cannot be valid unless the child was at least six weeks old when it was given. This provision is intended to prevent a mother making a vital decision regarding her child's future at a time when she may not have fully recovered from her confinement. All consents are revocable right up to the last moment before an adoption order is made. Under the old law a consent could be conditional upon the child being brought up in a particular religion, though once an adoption order was made there was no way by which this could be enforced. This provision has been repealed but adoption agencies placing children for adoption must have regard to the wishes of the natural parent concerning religious upbringing(Children Act 1975, s.13 [Adoption Act 1976 s.7]).

Faced with the refusal or withdrawal of a necessary consent of the impossibility of obtaining it due to the disappearance or disability of any parent or guardian, applicants for adoption can apply to a court for an order dispensing with any consent which is required. The grounds on which a court can make such an order are listed in the Children Act 1975 s.12 [Adoption Act 1976, s.16] and are:

(a) *That the parent or guardian in question "cannot be found or is incapable of giving agreement"*

An illustration of this ground is the case of *Re R. (Adoption)* (1967) which concerned the proposed adoption of a boy who was a national of a country under a totalitarian regime from which he had escaped illegally. His parents were both alive and still living in that country but any attempt to communicate with them by letter or private intermediary or through British diplomatic or consular offices would have exposed them to embarrassment and danger. Accordingly they were not given notice of the proposed adoption of their son, and an application was made to dispense with their consent, which was successful for the following reasons:

> "If the circumstances are such that there are no practical means of communication so that there is no practical means of securing consent, then a person "cannot be found" . . . It can truly be said that they are incapable of giving their consent, for how can a man consent to a proposal of which he is ignorant and cannot, as a practical matter, be made aware?" (*per* Buckley J).

(b) *That the parent or guardian in question "has abandoned, neglected or persistently ill-treated" the child whose adoption is sought*

This ground has been narrowly interpreted by the courts so that only abandonment, neglect or ill-treatment of a kind and degree amounting to a criminal offence enables the judge to dispense with any consent on this ground. Thus in *Watson* v. *Nikolaisen* (1955) a mother was held not to have abandoned her child, and her consent was accordingly not dispensed with, although she had handed her child shortly after its birth to friends together with a consent for its adoption in proper form and had afterwards never visited or taken any interest whatsoever in the child until the friends three years later applied for adoption, when she withdrew her consent. (However, this case would now come under heading (c), below)

(c) *That the parent or guardian in question "is withholding his agreement unreasonably"*

This is the most common ground relied upon in applications of this kind. The welfare of the child has not traditionally been the sole consideration in dispensing with consent under this heading. The rights of parents also have to be considered. Before the passing of the Children Act 1975 there was considerably controversy on this, many people feeling that the welfare of the child should be the paramount consideration, others feeling that if this were so unfortunate parents who were, for no fault of their own, unable to look after their children for the time being, for example because of homelessness, would be in danger of having their children adopted without their consent. Accordingly a compromise formula was adopted in section 3 of the 1975 Act [Adoption Act 1976, s.6] which enacted that the court, in reaching any decision relating to the adoption of a child shall give "first consideration" to the need to safeguard and promote the welfare of the child." However, in *Re P.* (1977) the Court of Appeal held that this section does not apply when the court is deciding whether or not to dispense with a parent's consent on the ground that it is being withheld unreasonably. The law on this, therefore, is still the same as it was before the Children Act was passed, and the welfare of the child is not the first consideration in making these decisions. Nevertheless, the welfare of the child has been and will continue to be a most important consideration as can be seen from the following leading cases decided in the House of Lords. In *Re W.* (1971) the mother of an illegitimate child opposed his adoption by foster parents with whom he had lived since birth in 1968. The mother, whose home life was unstable, was in no way blameworthy, nevertheless the need for her consent was dispensed with on the ground that it was unreasonably withheld. Lord Hailsham said,

" . . . it is clear that the test is reasonableness and not anything else. It is not culpability. It is not indifference. It is not failure to discharge parental duties . . . But, although welfare *per se* is not the test, the fact that a reasonable parent does pay regard to the welfare of his child must enter into the question of reasonableness as a relevant factor. It is relevant in all cases if and to the extent that a reasonable parent would take it into account. It is decisive in those cases where a reasonable parent must so regard it."

In *O'Connor* v. *A. and B.* (1971) an illegitimate child had been placed with prospective adopters with the consent of the mother. She later refused her consent as she had married the child's father. The parents' consent was dispensed with. The court recognised the strength of the claim of the parents who were married to each other and able to provide a home, but nevertheless considered that in the circumstances of the case (and especially the fact that the child had been cared for by the prospective adopters for two and a half years) the welfare of the child should prevail.

The court will rarely dispense with the consent of a natural parent if it is clear that the child will in any case remain living with the prospective adopters and the only reason for the adoption is to cut out the natural parent (*e.g.* where a mother and stepfather wish to terminate contact with the child's natural father, *Re B.* (1975)).

However in the disturbing case of *Re D*. (1977) the House of Lords did dispense with the natural father's consent because he was homosexual and had "nothing to offer his son at any time in the future."

(d) *That the parent or guardian in question "has persistently failed without reasonable cause to discharge the parental duties in relation to the child"*

The obligations of a parent or guardian to be considered include "the natural and moral duty of a parent to show affection, care and interest towards his child and the common law and statutory duty of a parent to maintain his child in the financial or economic sense" (*Re P*. (1962)).

(e) *That the parent has seriously ill-treated the child and the rehabilitation of the child in the parents' household is unlikely*

This new ground is designed to deal with the situation where a parent has committed an isolated act of violence, against a child and thus cannot be considered to have "persistently" ill-treated him under heading (b) above, and the child is likely to be ill-treated again if he is returned to the parent.

5. Freeing a child for adoption

A new procedure concerning adoption has been introduced by the Children Act 1975 but is not yet in force. It is designed to take some of the uncertainty and distress out of the procedure relating to parental consent. At the moment a mother will often give her child for adoption at birth, but she will be unable to consent formally until the child is six weeks old. Later she will be interviewed by the guardian *ad litem* to see if she still fully consents. She is constantly aware that she may revoke her consent and if the arrangements for the adoption fall through she will have to consent again to any application by new adopters. This is very unsettling to a mother who has decided from the beginning to consent to adoption. It is also very unsettling for the prospective adopters who will be constantly aware that the mother might withhold her consent.

Accordingly under section 14 [Adoption Act 1976, s.18] an adoption agency will be able to apply to a court for an order freeing a child for adoption with the consent of the parents, or for an order that the parental consent may be dispensed with in adoption proceedings. The effect of the order is to vest parental rights and duties in the adoption agency. The agency may then arrange for an adoption and the natural parent is not concerned any more in these arrangements. The natural parents' consent to the actual adoption which is eventually arranged is not needed. A parent can make a declaration that he does not wish to be involved in any future questions concerning his child's adoption. If he does not do this then the adoption agency must inform the parent 12 months after the order freeing the child for adoption has been made whether or not the child has been adopted or placed for adoption. If neither of these has taken place the parent can then apply for a revocation of the order on the ground that he wishes to resume parental rights and duties.

6. Duties and powers of local authorities

Local authorities already have powers to arrange adoption. Moreover notice of all proposed adoptions must be sent to the relevant local authority. The child then becomes a "protected child" who should be visited from time to time by an officer of the authority who should satisfy himself on the child's well-being and give such advice as may be needed. The Children Act 1975, s.1 makes it the duty of local authorities to establish comprehensive adoption services but this provision is not yet in force because of lack of resources. When it is implemented the local authority will be able, as part of their adoption service, to provide mother and baby homes, to arrange adoptions and to provide counselling for all involved in adoption.

The approval and supervision of independent adoption societies is done under the Children Act 1975 by the Minister and not by local authorities.

7. The Court's functions on making adoption orders

The Children Act 1975, s.3 [Adoption Act 1975, s.6] lays down the basic duty of the court. It must give first consideration to the welfare of the child in making any decision relating to that child's adoption. The court should also find out what are the wishes of the child, if this is practicable having regard to the child's age and understanding.

The main function of the court, apart from actually making the order, is to ensure that all the conditions for adoption have been complied with, for example that any consents have been freely and properly given and that no payment has been offered, asked for or made in connection with the adoption.

Applicants for adoption have a choice of courts as the High Court, county courts and magistrates' courts have overlapping jurisdiction to make adoption orders. The High Court is very rarely chosen for this purpose and at the present time about two-thirds of all orders are made in county courts. Application is made on a printed form which, after having been duly filled in, is lodged at the court with some additional prescribed documents including whatever consents have been obtained. Prospective adopters may opt to keep their identity and address a secret from the natural parents of the child and generally do so.

Application to the court at the moment automatically leads to the appointment of a guardian *ad litem* who is usually either a probation officer or a children's officer of a local authority. His duty is to make a thorough and completely independent investigation of the history, circumstances and merits of the proposed adoption in accordance with the requirements of the Adoption Rules. These include interviews with all parties concerned and visits to the adopters' home to observe the child's progress and the adopters' attitudes towards it. The guardian's written report about his inquiries is in due course carefully considered by the judge before making his decision regarding the proposed adoption order. When the Children Act 1975, s.20 [Adoption Act 1975, s.65] is in operation the appointment of a guardian *ad litem* will not be automatic but only in such cases as will be provided in rules of court. It is envisaged that in most cases where the adoption is arranged by a local authority or agency a guardian *ad litem* will not be needed, as in general he merely repeats the work already done by the agency.

The hearing takes place in private without publicity. It is attended by the adopters and any children they may have, the child to be adopted, the guardian and sometimes other adoption workers who have taken part in the arrangements for the adoption. Legal representation is very rare in a county or juvenile court. The length and character of the hearing, which is completely informal, depend on the personality of the judge. All procedural or other technical problems which may have presented themselves should have been dealt with on earlier interlocutory applications so that, provided the judge considers the proposed order to be for the welfare of the child, the hearing is a happy occasion for all concerned. In making an adoption order a judge may impose such terms and conditions as he thinks fit (Children Act 1975, s.8(7) [Adoption Act 1976, s.12(6)]. In recent cases adoption orders have actually been made subject to provision for access by natural parents under this provision. This is obviously only done in exceptional circumstances as adoption should mean a complete break between natural parent and child (see *Re J.* (1973) and *Re S.* (1976)). If not satisfied, a judge may adjourn an application or make an interim order giving the applicants custody for a period not exceeding two years. If an adoption order is refused, the child must be returned to the society or local authority which introduced it within seven days.

After the making of an adoption order full particulars are transmitted by he court to the office of the Registrar General, which leads to the entry in the register of births relating to the birth of the adopted child being marked "Adopted" and to the particulars of the adoption order being entered in the Adopted Children Register. A new birth certificate recording the fact of adoption is then issued to the adopted child. At the General Register Office confidential records are kept which enable the connection between an entry of birth and the corresponding entry in the Adopted Children Register to be established. Provision has been made under the Children Act 1975, s.26 [Adoption Act 1976, s.5] for an adopted person over 18 to apply to the Registrar General for a copy of his original birth certificate. As the information contained on that certificate might come as a shock to the adopted person (or as a shock to his natural parent who might as a consequence be traced by his child) the Act requires the Registrar General to provide information of counselling services available to the applicant. Such counselling is compulsory for all those adopted before the passing of the Children Act because in many of those cases natural parents have been assured by adoption workers that their child would never be able to trace them.

8. Convention Adoptions

The Adoption Act 1968 [Adoption Act 1976, s.17] gives effect to the convention relating to the adoption of children which was concluded and signed on behalf of the United Kingdom in 1965. It enables "a qualified person" or "qualified spouses," although not domiciled in England or Scotland, to apply to the High Court for an adoption order under this Act, which has broadly the same effect as an adoption order under the Children Act 1975, s.8. A "qualified person," able to use this procedure instead of applying for a provisional order under the Act of 1958, is any person, other than a national of the United Kingdom or of a country to which the convention applies, who is habitually resident in Great Britain, or any national of the United Kingdom who is habitually resident in a foreign convention country of a specified British country.

CHAPTER 14

CHILDREN IN NEED

The responsibility for caring for children with no parents or guardian, or for neglected or ill-treated children lies with local authorities. A series of enactments, many now consolidated in the Child Care Act 1980 and the Foster Children Act 1980, have given wide powers and duties to local authorities to receive, take and keep children in care, or to supervise them whilst living at home. Whilst no one would deny that a local authority should care for a child who is being maltreated or who has no one else to look after him, there can be considerable controversy between parents and local authorities in cases where the real reason for the parent's inability to care for their children is poverty or lack of housing, or where the local authority objects to a parent's unconventional lifestyle. The legislation on care is often vague about the rights of both parents and children. It is also technical and complicated. For these reasons local authorities will sometimes prefer to use the wardship procedure rather than rely on their statutory powers. Parents have also found it advantageous to use this procedure but the decision in *A.* v. *Liverpool City Council* (1981) has considerably limited the utility of wardship from the parents' point of view (see p.122).

1. Basic duties of local authorities

The Child Care Act 1980, s.1. imposes a duty upon local authorities to promote the welfare of children in the following terms:

1(1) "It shall be the duty of every local authority to make available such advice, guidance and assistance as may promote the welfare of children by diminishing the need to receive children into or keep them in care under this Act or to bring children before a juvenile court; and any provisions made by a local authority under this subsection may, if the local authorities think fit, include provision for giving assistance in kind or, in exceptional circumstances, in cash.

(2) In carrying out their duty under subsection (1) above, a local authority may make arrangements with voluntary organisations or other persons for the provision by those organisations or other persons of such advice, guidance or assistance as is mentioned in that subsection."

Once a child is in the care of a local authority they must have regard to section 18 of the 1980 Act in discharging their duties:

"18(1) In reaching any decision relating to a child in their care, a local authority shall give first consideration to the need to safeguard and promote the welfare of the child throughout his childhood; and shall so far as practicable ascertain the wishes and feelings of the child regarding the decision and give due consideration to them, having regard to his age and understanding.

(2) In providing for a child in their care a local authority shall make such use of facilities and services available for children in the care of their own parents as appears to the local authority reasonable in his case."

In many ways these sections describe hopes and aspirations rather than impose legally enforceable duties. However they can have legal consequences. In *Tilley* v. *London Borough of Wandsworth* (1981) the local authority decided that as a matter of policy it would not exercise its powers under section 1, to give "assistance in kind or . . . in cash" in order to pay off the rent arrears or rehouse families in arrears with the rent. Instead the children would be taken into care on the eviction of the family. It was held that the council could not fetter its discretion under section 1 in this fashion. Each case had to be dealt with on its merits.

It is clear that the legislation encourages local authorities to make efforts to help families and avoid the need for receiving or keeping children in care. However despite this in 1980 about 100,000 children were in care. The rest of this chapter is concerned with the two main ways in which children come into and are kept in care, first under the Child Care Act 1980, and second under the Children and Young Persons Act 1969. Children can also be placed in care under other enactments, in particular under matrimonial legislation where there are "exceptional circumstances" (see pp.110–111).

2. Reception into care

A child under the age of 17 can be received into care by a local authority under section 2 of the Child Care Act 1980. This section imposes a *duty* upon local authorities to take in a child who:

   (i) has no parent or guardian,
   (ii) has been abandoned by his parent or guardian,
  (iii) is lost,
  (iv) whose parent or guardian is unable to care for him because of illness, incapacity or "any other circumstances."

In all cases the intervention of the local authority must be necessary in the interests of the child. This section was really designed to deal with emergencies (*i.e.* where a child is lost or its parents suddenly become homeless) and where the parents (if available) *consented* to their child being received into care. A local authority cannot *take* a child into care against its parents' wishes under this section. If the child is in danger and the parents will not consent to care then the local authority should seek a place of safety order, followed by a care order (see pp. 137–140). Accordingly section 2 also provides that the local authority should "endeavour to secure that the care of the child is taken over" by the parent, a relative or friend.

Section 2 also provides that "nothing in this section shall authorise a local authority to keep a child in their care ... if any parent or guardian desires to take over the care of the child ... " This provision has caused many problems. A parent may wish to reclaim his child in circumstances which the local authority consider against the child's best interests. This will often be the case where the child has been in care under section 2 for a long time, which, despite the essentially temporary nature of section 2 care, is sometimes the case. This problem is partly dealt with by section 13 of the 1980 Act which provides that where the child has been in care for six months or more the parent must give the local authority 28 days notice of his intention to take the child back.

It seems clear that if the parent demands the *immediate* return of his child and the child has been in care less than six months, then the local authority can no longer keep the child (*London Borough of Lewisham* v. *Lewisham Juvenile Court* (1980)). However it appears that they have no positive obligations to do anything to hand over the child to the parents (*Krishnan* v. *London Borough of Sutton* (1970)). The law on this is in a state of confusion despite the House of Lords decision of *Lewisham*. The best course of action, from the point of view of the local authority faced with a parental demand for the return of a child who has been in care under section 2 for less than six months, is to make the child a ward of court. (*Re C.* (1963); *Re S.* (1965); *A.* v. *Liverpool City Council* (1981)). The court can then make whatever order it thinks in the best interests of the child (see Chapter 12 for Wardship).

Where the child has been in section 2 care for over six months then, on being told that the parent wishes to take his child back, the local authority has 28 days in which to pass a resolution, under section 3 of the Child Care Act 1980, assuming full parental rights and duties, providing the conditions laid down in section 3 are satisfied.

3. Parental Rights resolutions

This is a procedure whereby, by an administrative decision, a local authority can assume full parental rights over a child and the parent then has no further rights to resume the care of or even have access to the child without the local authorities' consent.

The procedure can be used only where a child is already in voluntary care under section 2 of the Child Care Act, as described above. Where a child is in section 2 care and a parent has asked the local authority to return the child the local authority still has the power to pass a resolution under section 3. The child is regarded as being "in care under section 2" for as long as it remains in the actual custody of the local authority (*London Borough of Lewisham* v. *Lewisham Juvenile Court* (1980)).

The grounds upon which a local authority can pass a parental rights resolution under section 3 are as follows:

(a) that his parents are dead and he has no guardian or custodian, or

(b) that a parent—
  (i) has abandoned him, or
  (ii) suffers from a permanent disability so that he is incapable of caring for him, or
  (iii) suffers from a mental disorder which renders him unfit to care for the child, or
  (iv) has such habits or follows a mode of life making him unfit to care for him, or
  (v) has consistently failed without reasonable cause to discharge the obligations of a parent so as to be unfit to care for him, or

(c) that a resolution under (b) above is in force in relation to one parent of the child who is, or is about to become a member of the household of the other parent who is caring for the child, or

(d) that throughout the previous three years the child has been in the care of the local authority under section 1.

Where ground (b)(v) above is used it must be proved that the parent has been culpable to a fairly high degree in neglecting his or her child. Where she or he has been unable to look after the child because of misfortune or illness then this does not amount to failure "without reasonable cause" (*O'Dare A i* v. *Glamorgan* (1980); *Wheatley* v. *London Borough of Waltham Forest* (1979)).

Where the parent is alive and his or her whereabouts are known, he or she can consent in writing to the passing of the resolution. In such a case the parent cannot object after it has been passed, although he or she could challenge the validity of the resolution before the Divisional Court if it was *ultra vires* (*e.g.* where there was a procedural irregularity or some other failure to observe the law).

A parent who has not consented to the passing of the resolution must be told of it as soon as possible. He or she then has one month in which to object. If an objection is lodged the resolution will lapse after 14 days unless the local authority goes to the juvenile court. The court may either confirm or rescind the resolution. Unlike care proceedings (see below), the parent is the defendant in such proceedings and therefore entitled to legal aid. The child is not, yet, a party to the action but provision for making him a party and for providing a guardian *ad litem* is made in section 7 of the Child Care Act 1980. This section is not yet in force.

A valid resolution remains in force until a child's eighteenth birthday unless the local authority in the meantime rescinds it, if such action appears to them to be in the child's interest, or a juvenile court on a complaint by a parent or guardian discharges it on the same ground (*ibid.* s.5(4)). Provided a local authority has lawfully and in good faith assumed parental rights, a court will not, in wardship proceedings or in any other proceedings at the insistance of a parent normally interfere with a local authority's exercise of its powers (*A.* v. *Liverpool City Council* (1981)). However, the assumption of parental rights in respect of one parent only does not limit the rights of the other parent. Thus in *R.* v. *Oxford City Justices* (1975) the local authority had assumed the parental rights of the mother of an illegitimate child. The father therefore was still able to exercise his right to apply for custody under the Guardianship of Minors Act 1971.

4. Care proceedings

Where a local authority wishes to *take* child into care, irrespective of the parents' consent, it has to bring care proceedings in the juvenile court under the Children and Young Persons Act 1969, s.1. Care proceedings are normally begun by summons. However if the child is in danger they can be preceded by a "place of safety" order. This is a warrant issued by a magistrate to either a social worker or a police officer. The magistrate must be satisfied that the applicant has reasonable grounds for believing that one of the grounds (a)–(d) (*post*) for a care order exist in respect of the child (1969 Act, s.28). The child may then be taken to a place of safety, such as a community home, police station or hospital, for up to 28 days. The parents should be informed as soon as possible but there is little or nothing that they can realistically do to challenge a place of safety order or get their child returned. If the local authority wishes to continue to care for the child then it should apply to the juvenile court for a care order under section 1 of the 1969 Act as outlined below.

Grounds for care proceedings

Care proceedings can be begun by a local authority, the NSPCC or a police officer. Local authorities have a duty to do so if it appears to them that there are grounds for such proceedings in respect of a child or young person in their area, unless they are satisfied that it is neither in the child's or young person's nor the public interest that proceedings should be brought or that some other person is about to do so or to charge a young person with an offence (ss.1(1), 2(2)).

Grounds for instituting care proceedings in respect of a child or young person are that:

(a) his proper development is being avoidably prevented or neglected or his health is being avoidably impaired or neglected or he is being ill-treated, or

(b) a court has been satisfied that a child or young person who is or was a member of the same household has suffered in any of the above respects and it is probable that he will suffer likewise, or

(c) it is probable that condition (b) will be satisfied because a person who has been convicted of certain offences against the person (mentioned in Schedule of the 1933 Children and Young Persons Act) is or may become a member of the same household as the child, or

(d) he is exposed to moral danger, or

(e) he is beyond the control of his parent or guardian, or

(f) he is of compulsory school age and is not receiving efficient full-time education suitable to his age, ability and aptitude, or

(g) he is guilty of an offence (excluding homicide). (This ground applies only to children over 10 years old and is rarely used as a basis for care proceedings. Criminal proceedings (see *post*, p.140) will be preferred.

In addition it must be proved that the child is in need of care and control which he is unlikely to receive unless the court makes one of the orders (see below) available to it.

It should be noted that the local authority must in general prove that one of the above conditions exists at the time of the proceedings. It is not enough to maintain that the child *might be* exposed to moral danger, or *might be* or even is *likely to be* neglected or ill-treated (*J.B.R.* v. *Essex County Council* (1978)).

Orders that the court can make

If satisfied that one of the above conditions exists and that the child is in need of care and control the court can make one of the following orders:

1. An order requiring his parent or guardian to enter into a recognisance to take proper care of him and exercise proper control of him. Such an order can be made only with the parent's or guardian's consent.

2. A supervision order (1969 Act, ss.11–19). By such an order a child or young person is generally placed under the supervision of a local authority whose duty is, while the order is in force "to advise, assist and befriend" the supervised person. A supervision order may be made subject to various directions to the supervised person, which are liable to bring him back before the court if they are not obeyed. Unless previously discharged or made for a shorter period, a supervision order is valid for three years or, if it is earlier, until the eighteenth birthday of the supervised person.

3. A care order (ss. 20, 21, 24). Such an order commits a child or young person to the care of a local authority whose duty it is to receive him into their care and "notwithstanding any claim by his parent or guardian to keep him in their care" while the order is in force. During this period the local authority have the same powers and duties in respect of a person in their care as his parent or guardian would have apart from the order and, in particular, the authority is empowered to restrict his liberty to such an extent as the authority consider appropriate. The child might be sent to an appropriate community home, boarded out with foster parents or returned to its own parents, at the discretion of the local authority. Care orders are subject to variation and discharge just as are supervision orders, but unless previously discharged a care order is valid until a person attains the age of 18 or until the age of 19 if the order was made when the person to whom it relates had attained the age of 16.

4. A hospital order within the meaning of Part V of the Mental Health Act 1959.

5. A guardianship order within the meaning of the same Act. Either of the last orders is appropriate if the child or young person is within the scope of this Act by reason of mental disorder.

Appealing and legal aid

The child, or the parent on behalf of the child, can appeal against the making of an order to the Crown Court. The local authority has no right of appeal if an order is refused (1969 Act, s.2(12)). It should be noted that in care proceedings the *child* is the defendant and therefore entitled to legal aid. The parents are not parties and not, in general, entitled to legal aid. They are entitled to meet any allegations made against them during the hearing. The position of parents in care proceedings is therefore very unsatisfactory. Although provision was made in the Children Act 1975 to allow parents to be legally aided, it has not yet been brought into force except where the case concerns the *revocation* of a care order and is *undefended*. This apparently strange exception results from the inquiry into the death of Maria Colwell, a girl in care whose mother applied for the revocation of the order which was not contested by the local authority. The court, having no other evidence before it, revoked the care order and Maria returned to her mother's house where she was killed by her step-father. Maria herself did not wish to return to her mother but she was not separately represented before the court. Future Marias and their parents will be separately represented which should ensure that all the evidence is put before the court and properly tested.

5. Criminal proceedings

A child between 10–14, or a young person between 14–17 can be charged directly with a criminal offence before the juvenile court. (The provision contained in the Children and Young Persons Act 1969 to raise the age of criminal responsibility to 14 has never been brought into force). It was the intention of the framers of the 1969 legislation that most children who were alleged to have committed a crime should be dealt with in care proceedings but the reverse in fact happened. It is clear also that criminal proceedings are frequently begun by the Police without first consulting the local social services department, another of the aims of the 1969 Act.

One of the reasons for the continuing popularity of criminal rather than care proceedings is that the court has wider powers in criminal proceedings. In addition to all the orders listed on p.139 which are available in care proceedings, the court can also impose a fine of up to £50 for a child or £200 for a young person (and in some cases order a parent to pay it), make a compensation order, give a conditional discharge, make an attendance centre order or a detention centre order. In addition the court may remit the case of a juvenile over 15 years old to the Crown Court with a view to imposing a borstal training order. A care order should be made in criminal proceedings only for an offence for which an adult offender would be imprisoned.

Juveniles accused of crime are subject to special rules in relation to arrest, questioning and fingerprinting which are beyond the scope of this book.

INDEX

Access, 109
  agreements and, 52
  care and, 122
  custodianship, on, 113
  grandparents, by, 58
  magistrates' courts in, 57
  refusal to parent, 109
  right of child, 109
Adoption, 124
  agencies, 126
  consents, 126
  consent of court, 126–129
  consent of parents, 105
  consent of putative father, 119
  convention, 132
  courts' powers, 130
  effect of order, 124
  freeing for, 129
  guardian *ad litem*, 131
  legislation on, 124
  local authority powers, 130
  married couples, by, 125
  parents, by, 125
  private placements, 126
  procedure, 131
  prohibited degrees and, 5
  protected child, 125, 130
  registration of, 132
  refusal of consent to, 126–129
  revocation of, 124
  single persons, by, 125
  step parents, by, 125
  who may be adopted, 125
Adultery,
  cohabitation and, 66
  damages for, 17
  intolerability, 65, 66
  maintenance and, 18
  meaning, 65
  polygamy and, 13
  proof, 66
Affiliation, 117
  corroboration, 118

Affiliation—*cont.*
  criteria for order, 118
  duration of order, 118
  lump sum, 117
  maintenance on, 117
  single women, 117
Affinity,
  bar to marriage, 5
Age,
  care and, 134
  criminal responsibility, of, 140
  marriage, for, 4
Agency,
  household, 18
  necessity, of, 18
Agreements,
  maintenance for children, 97
  separation. *See* Separation
      Agreements.
  access and, 52
Attachment of Earnings, 59

Bank Accounts, 28
Banns, 8
Behaviour,
  cohabitation and, 68
  cruelty and, 67
  illness and, 67, 68
  magistrates' courts in, 55
  meaning, 67
Bigamy, 6
  validity of marriage and, 6
Blood Tests, 115
Breakdown of Marriage. *See*
      Divorce.

Capacity,
  marriage, for, 4
Care. *See also* Care Proceedings.
  access and, 122
  domestic proceedings in, 58
  local authority duties, 133

Care—*cont.*
  marriage of child in, 8
  order, 139
  parental rights resolution, 135
  parent's demand for child, 135
  parents' rights, 137
  place of safety, 135, 137
  powers of local authority, 139
  procedure on, 136, 137
  reception into, 134
  revocation of order, 140
  voluntary, 134–5
  wardship and, 122, 133, 137
Care Proceedings,
  appeal, 140
  grounds for, 138
  legal aid, 139
  orders, 138–139
  procedure, 137
Child of the Family, 74, 95
Children. *See* Custody, Care,
  Access, Illegitimacy.
Cohabitation, 11
  affiliation, 117
  contract for, 12
  custody agreements, 107
  family provision and, 36–37
  fatal accidents, 112
  home and, 24
  household agency, 19
  housekeeping, 28
  housing rights, 11, 12
  inheritance, 11
  injunctions, 11, 28
  property disputes, 20
  Rent Acts and, 11
  supplementary benefit, 11
  tax, 12, 30, 31
  tenancies and, 27
Consanguinity,
  bar to marriage, 5
Consents,
  adoption, to, 105, 126
  blood tests, to, 116
  insanity and, 116
  marriage, to, 7, 8, 82, 84, 106
  medical treatment, to, 105, 106
  putative father, of, 119

Consortium, 16
Contract,
  cohabitation, 12
  married women, 39
  separation, on. *See* Separation
    Agreement.
  spouses between, 39
Crime,
  care proceedings and, 138
  evidence, 40, 41
  juveniles and, 140
  offences against children, 106
  orders, on, 140
  spouses, between, 40
  wife's statutory defence, 40
Custodianship, 112
Custody,
  agreements and, 12, 52, 107
  custodianship, 112
  defined, 106–107
  divorce, on, 74, 110
  father's rights, 107
  grandparents to, 109
  joint, 107, 110, 111
  magistrates' courts, in, 57, 111
  mother's rights, 107
  parental right to, 106
  principles of, 107–109
  putative fathers and, 118
  step parents, 113
  third parties and, 57, 109, 112
  wardship and, 120–122

Death,
  divorce on presumption of, 6
  family provision, 33, 34
  fatal accidents, 37
  guardianship, on, 112
  intestacy, 33
  surviving spouse and, 34
  survivorship, 28
  wills, 33
Desertion, 17, 68
  consent and, 70
  magistrates' courts in, 55, 56
  separate households, 69
  separation, 69

Divorce,
adultery. *See* Adultery.
appeal, 77
arrangements for children, 74, 110
behaviour. *See* Behaviour.
custody on, 110
decree absolute, 74, 77
decree *nisi*, 77
defences, 72
defended, 63, 76
desertion, and. *See* Desertion.
exceptional hardship, 64
financial protection on, 72, 75
foreign decrees, 100–102
ground for, 65
other hardship, 73
polygamous marriages and, 13
presumption of death on, 6
procedure, 76–77
proof, 65
reconciliation, 64
separation. *See* Separation.
special procedure, 76
talaq, 100
within three years of marriage, 63
Domestic Violence. *See under*
Injunctions.
Domicile, 13, 14, 100
Duress,
nullity, in, 82

Education,
care proceedings and, 138
parental duty to, 105
Enforcement,
arrest powers, 48, 49
attachment of earnings, 59
committal, 60
magistrates' courts, in, 58–61
Engagements,
capacity, 4
gifts, 3, 4
legal effect, 3
property on, 3
Enticement, 17
Evidence,
affiliation proceedings, in, 118

Evidence—*cont.*
blood tests, 115
spouses of, 40, 41
wardship in, 120
Exclusion Order, 48
arrest, 49

Family Provision, 34–37
criteria for, 35
dependants for, 36
powers of court, 36
Fatal Accidents,
assessment of damages, 38
cohabitants, 12, 37, 38
dependants' claims, 37
Financial Provision. *See under*
Maintenance, Matrimonial
Home, Matrimonial Property.
Foreign decrees,
public policy and, 101
recognition of, 100–103
Formalities,
defective, 10

Gifts,
engagement, 3, 4
home, of, 22
spouses, between, 29
wedding, 29
Grandparents,
access and, 58
custody, 109
Guardian *ad litem*,
adoption in, 131
care in, 137
Guardianship, 112

Harbouring, 17
Housekeeping Money, 18, 29

Illegitimacy, 12, 114
affiliation. *See* Affiliation.
care and, 137
consent to marriage, 8
custody and, 118
custody agreements, 107
defined, 114
mother's rights, 105

Illegitimacy—*cont.*
  prohibited degrees and, 5
  proof of paternity, 115
  voidable marriages, 114
  void marriages, 114
Injunctions,
  arrest and, 48
  cohabitants, 11, 47
  county court, 45
  criteria for, 46
  enforcement, 48
  ex parte, 48
  jurisdiction, 46
  magistrates' court, 48
  ouster, 45
  property rights, and, 47

Judicial Separation, 77
  arrangements for children, 110
  polygamy and, 13

Legal Aid, 61
  care proceedings, 139
  parental rights resolutions, 137
Legitimacy, 114
  declaration of, 116
  presumption of, 115
Local Authorities,
  care proceedings, 137
  duties to children, 133

Magistrates' Courts, 54
  access in, 57
  appeals, 62
  consent order, 55
  custody in, 111
  enforcement of order, 58
  grounds in, 55, 56
  jurisdiction, 54
  legal aid in, 61
  lump sums, 56
  maintenance, 56
  powers, 55
  press and, 61
  procedure, 61
  registration in, 61
  variation of order, 58
  welfare reports, 111

Maintenance, 49, 87
  adultery and, 18
  agreements and, 51
  attachment of earnings, 59
  avoiding transactions, 99
  children for, 52, 56, 57, 87, 91, 93,
      95–97, 106, 117
  clean break, 91
  common law, at, 17
  conduct, 90
  credit and, 18
  direct to child, 93
  duration of, 88
  during marriage, 18
  illegitimate child of, 117
  length of marriage, 90
  lump sums, 56, 87, 88, 92
  magistrates' courts in, 55, 56
  neglect to, 19
  nullity on, 86, 87
  one-third rule, 89
  pre-marital cohabitation, 91
  principles of, 88
  prison and, 60
  reciprocal enforcement, 102
  registration in magistrates'
      courts, 61
  resources, 91
  responsibilities, 91
  secured, 88
  small maintenance payments, 94
  supplementary benefit, 92, 94
  tax and, 92
  undertakings, 88
  variation of, 61, 98
  wife's earnings, 92
Marriage,
  age for, 4
  Banns of, 8
  bigamy and, 6
  capacity, 4
  ceremony, 9, 10
  Church of England, in, 8
  civil, 9
  common law, 11
  common licence, 9
  consents to, 105
  consortium, 16

Marriage—*cont.*
  court's consent to, 8
  defective formalities, 7, 10
  definition, 3
  duty to cohabit, 16
  foreign, 3, 12
  formalities, 6
  limping, 100
  other churches, 9
  parental consent, 7
  polygamous, 12
  presumption of, 10
  prohibited degrees, 5
  reforms of procedure, 10
  registered building, 10
  special licence, 9
  superintendent registrar's
    certificate, 9
Matrimonial Home, 19
  See also Matrimonial Property.
  agreement, 21
  constructive trust, 22
  contributions to, 22
  beneficial interest, 23
  eviction from, 25, 28
  gift of, 22
  improvements to, 24
  injunctions, 28
  occupation of, 24, 45
  ownership, 21
  possession proceedings, 26
  registered land, 27
  registration of interest in, 25, 26,
    27
  rent of, 28
  resulting trust, 22
  sale of, 26, 87
  third parties and, 26
  transfer of tenancy, 27
  transfer on divorce, 97
  trust for sale, 26
Matrimonial Property, 19
  See also Matrimonial Home.
  bank accounts, 28
  bankruptcy and, 30
  death, on, 33
  defeating claims to, 49
  gifts, 29

Matrimonial Property—*cont.*
  housekeeping, 28, 29
  money, 28
  presumption of advancement, 30
  principles, 20–21
  procedure on dispute, 20
  savings, 29
  settlement of, 87
  survivorship, 28
  tax and, 30, 31
  transfer on divorce, 19
Medical Treatment,
  consent to, 105, 106

Necessaries,
  agency and, 18
Nullity, 79
  approbation of marriage, 85
  arrangements for children, 110
  defence, 81
  duress, 82
  impotence, 80
  insanity, 84
  jurisdiction, 86
  lack of consent, 82
  legitimacy and, 114
  mistake, 84
  need for decree, 79, 80
  pregnancy *per alium*, 85
  procedure, 86
  time limits, 85
  under age, 4, 79
  venereal disease, 85
  voidable marriages, 79, 80
  void marriages, 79
  wilful refusal to consummate, 81

Official Solicitor, 116, 120

Parental Rights,
  defined, 105
Paternity,
  declaration of, 116
  proof of, 115
Personal Protection Orders, 48
Place of Safety,
  order, 135, 137
Polygamy, 12, 80

Prohibited Degrees, 5
Protected Child, 125, 130
Putative Father,
    consent to adoption, of, 119
    custody, 118

Recognisance,
    care proceedings in, 139
Restitution of Conjugal Rights, 16

Separation,
    consent, 70, 71
    desertion in, 69
    five years, 71
    two years, 70
Separation Agreements, 51
    children, 52
    termination, 53
    terms, 51, 52
    validity, 51
    variation, 52
Services,
    damages for loss of, 17
    right to wife's, 17
Social Security. *See also*
    Supplementary Benefit.
    cohabitation rule, 32
    family income supplement, 32
    married women, 31, 32
    spouses and, 31
Step-parents,
    adoption by, 125

Supervision Orders, 57
    care proceedings, 139
Succession. *See* Death.
Supplementary Benefit,
    cohabitation, 11, 32
    diversion procedure, 61
    grave hardship and, 74
    liable relative, 32, 94
    lump sums and, 95
    maintenance and, 92, 94
    polygamy and, 13

Tax,
    capital gains, 31
    cohabitants and, 12, 30, 31
    divorce on, 92
    maintenance and, 92
    mortgage interest, 31
    separation on, 92
    small maintenance payments, 94
    spouses and, 30
    unearned income, 31
Tort,
    spouses and, 40

Wardship, 120
    care and, 122, 133
    contempt and, 121
    jurisdiction, 123
    kidnapping and, 123
    powers of court, 121
    procedure, 120
Wills. *See* Death.